. *World Famous* .

ROBBERIES

Colin Wilson, Damon Wilson and Rowan Wilson

MAGPIE
London

Magpie Books Ltd
7 Kensington Church Court
London W8 4SP

First published in the UK 1994
Copyright © Magpie Books Ltd
Illustrations and cover pictures © Popperfoto

ISBN 1 85813 389 0

Typeset by Hewer Text Composition Services, Edinburgh
Printed in Finland by
Werner Söderström Oy

CONTENTS

"IF YOU THINK TODAY IS LAWLESS . . ."

When we complain about the rising crime rate, we speak as citizens who take the protection of the law for granted. Police patrol our streets and country lanes. Burglary and mugging may be on the increase; but at least the robbers take their freedom into their hands every time they set out to commit a crime.

If we are to understand the history of the past three thousand years we have to make an effort of imagination, and try to forget this notion of being protected by the law. In ancient Greece, the problem was not simply the brigands who haunted the roads and the pirates who infested the seas; it was the fact that the ordinary citizen became a brigand or pirate when he felt like it, and no one regarded this as abnormal. In the *Odyssey*, Ulysses describes with pride how, on the way home from Troy, his ship was driven near to the coast of Thrace; so they landed near an unprotected town, murdered all the men, and carried off the women and goods. Greece was not at war with Thrace; it was just that an unprotected town was fair game for anyone, and the war-weary Greeks felt like a little rape and plunder. This state of affairs persisted for most of the next three thousand years, and explains why so many Mediterranean towns and villages are built inland.

What is far more difficult to grasp is that "law abiding" countries like England were in exactly the same situation. Just before the time of the Black Death (as Luke Owen Pike describes in his *History of Crime in England,* 1873), "houses were set on fire day after day; men and women were captured, ransom was exacted on pain of death . . . even those who paid it might think themselves fortunate if they escaped some horrible mutilation." And this does not relate to times of war or social upheaval; according to J.F. Nicholls and John Taylor's *Bristol Past and Present* (1881) England was "prosperous in the highest degree; populous, wealthy and luxurious . . ." (p. 174). Yet the robber bands were like small armies. They would often descend on a town when a fair was taking place and everyone felt secure; they would take over the town, plunder the houses and set them on fire (for citizens who were trying to save their houses would not organize a pursuit) and then withdraw. In 1347–8, Bristol was taken over by a brigand who robbed the ships in the harbour – including some commissioned by the King – and issued his own proclamations like a conqueror. His men roamed the streets, robbing and killing as they felt inclined – the King had to send Thomas, Lord Berkeley, to restore order. When a trader was known to have jewels belonging to Queen Philippa in his house, he was besieged by a gang led by one Adam the Leper and had to hand over the jewels when his house was set on fire. The law courts were almost powerless: when a notorious robber was tried near Winchester, the gang waited outside the court and attacked everyone who came out; the case was dropped.

The Age of Gin

Around the year 1650, a Dutch professor of chemistry called Sylvius discovered that a powerful alcohol could be made by distilling corn mash – which was cheap – and a sharp and pleasant flavour could be given it with juniper berries. This drink was called "geneva" (French for juniper), and this was soon shortened to gin.

It was sold in small bottles in chemists' shops, and the Dutch soon realized that geneva was as potent as good brandy, and far cheaper. When William and Mary installed themselves on James's throne in 1688, their countrymen began to export the new drink to England. Since England was quarrelling with France, and was therefore reluctant to buy French brandy, geneva – or gin – quickly became the national drink. Because of the brandy embargo, a law was passed permitting anyone to distil his own drink, and the English soon improved on the Dutch original, distilling an even cheaper grade of corn mash, and producing a powerful spirit that would now be called

The most famous of British highwaymen, Dick Turpin, never actually made the famous ride to York on his mare Bonnie Black Bess. Neither was he the courteous and heroic outlaw depicted by legend.

Born in 1705, Turpin was a butcher who turned to sheep-stealing to stock his shop. Inevitably found out, he lived by robbery and petty theft until he joined the notorious Essex Gang in 1735. One of his two quoted utterances is to a widow who refused to divulge the whereabouts of her cash: "God damn you, you old bitch, if you won't tell us I'll set your arse on the grate." On another occasion the gang poured boiling water over a farmer – whose skull they had cracked – while they took it in turns to rape his maid.

The gang was finally betrayed in an alehouse when a reward of a hundred guineas was offered for each, but Turpin escaped by jumping out of a window. It was after this that he took up highway robbery in Epping Forest, soon becoming one of the most successful highwaymen in the country. Hiding out in a cave, he murdered a keeper who tracked him down.

Turpin retired on his ill-gotten gains and settled in Yorkshire, calling himself John Palmer. He was arrested for shooting a gamecock and sheep-stealing, but no one suspected his identity. Turpin wrote to his brother from prison in York, asking for help, but sent the letter without a stamp. His brother failed to recognize the handwriting and refused to pay the postman sixpence. But a local schoolmaster caught a glimpse of the letter, recognised the handwriting of his old pupil and claimed the £200 reward on Turpin's head. Turpin was tried and sentenced to be hanged.

In jail he became a celebrity, receiving many visitors. One of them swore he was not Turpin, whereupon Turpin told a jailer "Lay him a wager and I'll go you halves", his only other recorded utterance.

On the scaffold, he preferred to launch himself into eternity by jumping from the ladder.

moonshine. (It is also probably a safe bet that this was when someone discovered that beer could be distilled to produce whisky.) Gin shops opened all over England – one London street had six of them.

Queen Elizabeth's subjects had drunk sherry (Falstaff's "sack"), beer and wine, which were cheap – wine cost fourpence a quart. Then James I had succeeded in raising some of the money Parliament refused to grant him by taxing various commodities, including wine and sherry, so that the English working man of the seventeenth century could only afford beer. By 1688, the English working classes were alcohol-starved. The consumption of gin rose steadily, from half a million gallons around 1690 to three and a half million by 1727 and to nineteen million gallons by the middle of the century.

The result was a crime wave. Many gin shops carried the notice: "Drunk for a penny, dead drunk for twopence, clean straw for nothing." Crimes to obtain money for gin became as common as crimes to obtain money for drugs in our own society. Theft became so common that, in 1699, a particularly savage act was passed that made almost any theft punishable by hanging, provided the goods were worth more than five shillings. At the same time, anyone who helped to secure the apprehension of a thief could obtain various tax exemptions and rewards. The measures were desperate; but so was the situation. Quite suddenly, England was virtually in a state of war with criminals. The diarist Narcissus Luttrell mentions an endless series of highway robberies and similar crimes. On one Saturday in 1693, a highwayman named Whitney had been arrested after resisting for an hour, and another highwayman was arrested in St Martin's Church. A gang of seven broke into Lady Reresby's house in Gerard Street, tied her and her family up and then rifled the house. Three coaches were robbed coming from Epsom, and three rowdies had caused an affray in Holborn, broken windows and run a watchman through with a sword, leaving it in his body. The invasion of houses by robber gangs had become as common as it was before the Black Death. A few years later, the famous robber Dick Turpin – whose exploits were far less romantic than his legend – led a gang that specialized in breaking into country houses, torturing the householders to force them to disclose valuables and raping any maids. Turpin's fame rested on the flamboyant manner of his death, bowing and waving to the mob from his cart, and finally voluntarily leaping from the gallows ladder.

All this makes an interesting contrast with crime in the age of
Queen Elizabeth. It had been just as widespread, but far less
serious. London was then full of thieves and confidence men
(known as "cony catchers", a cony being a rabbit). The thieves
used to meet once a week in the house of their leader, who also
happened to be the brother-in-law of the hangman; there, like
an aldermen's meeting, they discussed "prospects" and ex-
changed information. In contemporary descriptions (Robert
Greene wrote several pamphlets about it), the London criminal
scene in the time of Elizabeth sounds rather like Damon
Runyan's New York, deplorable but fairly good-natured. A
century later, this had changed. Highwaymen infested the
country roads, burglars operated in the towns, and women
and children appeared in the courts as frequently as men.
Children were trained as pickpockets, and were also sent
out to earn gin money by prostitution – the novelist Henry
Fielding, who became a magistrate in 1740, wrote of the large
number of children "eaten up with the foul distemper". The
government's reaction was to execute almost every offender
who appeared in court. In 1722, a gang of Hampshire poachers
had murdered a keeper who had interrupted them; they had

Black Bess and Dick Turpin (1706–39)

blackened their faces so as to be less visible in the dark. Landowners in the Waltham area (where it took place) were so alarmed that the government was prevailed upon to pass an act – the "Waltham Black Act" – which enabled almost any poacher to be hanged. (If the act had been in existence when Shakespeare was arrested for poaching from Sir Thomas Lucy, his works would have remained unwritten.) The act included a list of more than three hundred other offences – including catching rabbits – for which a man could be hanged.

Yet these measures had no effect on the rising crime rate. They could hardly be expected to when a large proportion of the population was permanently drunk. Henry Fielding reckoned that a hundred thousand people in London alone lived mainly on gin. Another observer stood outside a gin palace for three hours one evening and counted 1,411 people going in and out. These "palaces" usually consisted of a shed, full of barrels of gin; the customers merely came to buy a pennyworth of gin, which explains the enormous number. Whole families, including, father, mother and children, then sat on the pavement and drank themselves unconscious; with gin at a penny a quart, it was not difficult. The artist William Hogarth engraved two famous pictures, "Beer Street" and "Gin Lane", to expose the evil. In Beer Street, a lot of jolly-looking men and women are drinking outside a tavern and obviously engaging in intelligent political discussion (there is a copy of the king's speech on the table). In Gin Lane, a drunken mother allows her baby to fall out of her arms into the area below, a madman impales a baby on a spit, and a man who has hanged himself can be seen through the window of a garret. Fielding remarked that the gin "disqualifies them from any honest means to acquire it, at the same time that it removes sense of fear and shame and emboldens them to commit every wicked and dangerous enterprise." The result was that pickpockets who had once relied on skill and light fingers now knocked down their victims with bludgeons in broad daylight. The novelist Horace Walpole was shot in the face by a highwayman in Hyde Park in 1752.

Punishments, both in England and on the continent, had always been barbarous; now they became sadistic. The sentence of being hanged, drawn and quartered was usually reserved for political criminals, although it might be applied to some particularly violent robber. The victim was dragged to the place of execution behind a cart; he was then half-hanged, and his bowels were torn out while he was still alive and burned in front of him.

After this the body was cut into four pieces. Female criminals were often burned alive, because it was regarded as more "decent" than allowing them to risk exposing their private parts as they swung from a rope. (In this respect our ancestors were remarkably prudish.) But it was common for women – as well as men – to be stripped to the waist before being whipped through the streets to the pillory or gallows. After the 1699 act, thieves were branded on one cheek to make their offence public knowledge – this was probably regarded as an act of clemency, since most thieves were hanged. Prisoners accused of offences that involved speech – perhaps preaching false religious doctrines – would have a hole bored through the tongue as they were held in the pillory. A confidence man named Japhet Crook was sentenced to have both ears cut off and his nose slit open, then seared with a red hot iron. The hangman, known as 'Laughing Jack' Hooper, cut off both ears from behind with a sharp knife and held them aloft for the crowd to see, then cut

Ask anyone to name a famous pirate, and the chances are that they will say: "Captain Kidd". The truth is that Kidd was never a pirate.

William Kidd was a forty-year-old sea captain with a respectable record when the British government asked him to head a "privateering" expedition in 1695. A privateer plundered the ships of nations with whom his government was at war, and England was at that time at war with France. Kidd was also supposed to hunt real pirates – the unofficial variety – in the Red Sea.

Kidd captured and plundered two Armenian ships with French passes – which he was legally entitled to do – and the owners complained in London. When he arrived in New York, Kidd found to his astonishment that he had been proclaimed a pirate. He protested that he was nothing of the sort (and hid some of his loot), but when he ventured ashore he was arrested and returned to London. In the two years before he came to trial, the passes that would have proved his right to plunder the Armenian ships disappeared, and Kidd was convicted of piracy. He was also convicted of killing a member of his crew whom he had struck with a bucket – during a mutiny, he claimed. Kidd was hanged on 23 May 1701. The best known of all pirates was actually an innocent man.

open Crook's nostrils with scissors; however, when he applied the red hot iron to the bleeding nose, Crook leapt out of his chair so violently that Hooper – who was a kindly man – decided not to carry out the rest of the punishment. On the Continent, sentences were even crueller; red hot pincers were used to tear out the tongues of blasphemers. A madman called Damiens, who tried – rather half heartedly – to stab Louis XV of France in 1757, was executed by being literally "quartered". He was carried to the execution because his legs had been smashed with sledgehammers. His chest was torn open with red hot pincers, and lead poured into the wounds. Then his hands and feet were tied to four dray horses, which were whipped off in opposite directions. They were not strong enough to tear off his arms and legs, so more horses were brought; even so, the executioner had to partly sever the arms and legs before they could be pulled off. Damiens remained conscious until he had only one arm left – during the early part of the proceedings he looked on with apparent curiosity – and his hair turned white during the course of the execution.

The Theft of the Crown Jewels

Another villain who certainly deserved execution cheated the hangman because the King of England – Charles II – entirely lacked the spirit of vengefulness.

The infamous Colonel Blood was born in Sarney, County Meath, in Ireland, in 1618, and christened Thomas. His grandfather lived in Kilnaboy Castle, and was a Member of Parliament. Blood's father was a prosperous blacksmith who owned an ironworks. When the Civil War broke out in 1642, Blood hurried to England to fight on the side of King Charles I. But as it became clear that Cromwell's forces were going to win, he changed sides and joined the Roundheads. The result was that when Charles was defeated in 1653, Blood was made a Justice of the Peace and granted a large estate.

His prosperity lasted only seven years; when Charles II returned to the throne in 1660, Blood had to flee back to Ireland. He was not entirely destitute – he had married a

Lancashire heiress, who had borne him a son. In Ireland he joined a plot with other disgruntled Cromwellians to seize Dublin Castle and take its governor, Lord Ormonde, prisoner; it failed and he had to flee again, this time to Holland. After taking part in more political plots, he became a marked man with a price on his head. A daring rescue of a fellow conspirator, who was being taken to London under an escort of eight soldiers, again made Blood one of the most wanted men in the kingdom. In spite of this, he returned to England in 1670, and, under the name of Ayloffe, practised as a doctor at Romford.

He still dreamed of revenge on Lord Ormonde, who had dispossessed him and crushed his Irish plot. On 28 May 1670, Ormonde was on his way to a banquet in the Guildhall when he was held up in his coach and dragged out by several men. Blood then told him that he was going to be hanged at Tyburn, and sent the others off to prepare the gallows. But the coachman raised the alarm, and servants ran to Ormonde's aid; Blood fired a shot at him, then ran into the shadows of Piccadilly. (It was rumoured that he escaped with the aid of the Duke of Buckingham, who would have been glad to see Ormonde hanged.)

Back in Romford, he decided on an even bolder scheme: stealing the Crown Jewels, which were kept in the Tower of London, behind a grating in a locked basement room.

The keeper, Blood learned, was a man named Talbot Edwards, who lived with his family on the floor above the jewels. So one day early in 1671, disguised as a parson, Blood went to see the Crown Jewels, and became friendly with Talbot Edwards. Next time he went he took his wife. But as they were leaving the basement of the Martin Tower, Mrs Blood had a sudden violent stomach ache, and was taken into the Edwards' apartments to rest. The grateful Parson Blood returned a few days later with four pairs of white gloves for Mrs Edwards.

Blood was soon a regular visitor. And since Talbot Edwards had a pretty daughter, he was delighted when Blood proposed a match with his own wealthy nephew, an idea that his womenfolk also received with enthusiasm.

On 9 May 1671, Parson Blood arrived at 7 am with his "nephew" and two more companions. While the good-looking young man was making the acquaintance of the ladies, Blood suggested that they might see the Crown Jewels. Edwards thought it a good way of passing the time and led the way downstairs. He unlocked the door of the room that held the jewels, led them in, and locked it behind him. At that moment, he was knocked unconscious with a mallet wielded by Blood.

The thieves wrenched away the grating that protected the jewels, and removed the crown, orb and sceptre. The crown was flattened with the mallet and stuffed into a bag, the orb stuffed down the breeches of one of the men. Edwards, who had been tied up, began to struggle at this point, and Blood ran him through with his sword. The sceptre was too big to go into the bag, and one of the accomplices – Blood's brother-in-law, Hunt – began to file it through with a mallet.

Then there was an interruption. Edwards' son had been serving in Flanders, and he now arrived unexpectedly. Blood's "nephew", looking out of the window, saw him approaching and made an excuse to go downstairs. Blood decided that it was time to leave; they dropped the sceptre and hastened away.

At this moment, Edwards regained consciousness, and began to shout "Treason! Murder!". The son, now upstairs with his mother and sisters, ran down to see what was the matter. When he found his father bleeding from a sword wound, he raised the alarm.

Blood shot a sentry who tried to stop him, then made a minor mistake that betrayed loss of nerve: instead of leaving across the nearest drawbridge, by the Bulwark Gate, he changed his mind and made for the Iron Gate, near which his horse was tied. Even so, he came close to escape – the sentries mistook other guards for the fugitives and attacked them. Fortunately, the commander of the guard recognized the mistake, and reached Blood as he was mounting his horse. Blood pointed his pistol and pulled the trigger; it misfired. Beckman wrestled with Blood and finally overcame him. By this time the three accomplices had also been arrested.

In custody, Blood refused to answer questions, repeating stubbornly: "I'll answer to none but the King himself." Blood knew that the King had a reputation for liking bold scoundrels, and reckoned on his Irish charm to save his neck.

He proved correct. Blood was taken to the Palace, where he was questioned by the King, Prince Rupert, the Duke of York, and other members of the royal family. Charles was amused by his roguery, and chuckled when Blood remarked that his escapade had not been worth it, since the Crown Jewels were certainly not worth the £100,000 they were usually valued at – £6,000 would be nearer to it. Blood then went on to invent a tale of a plot to murder the King in which he himself had taken part. They had hidden, he explained, in the reeds at Battersea when the King went to the river to bathe, but "such was the awful majesty of your unclothed form that the weapon fell out of my hand." The King may have taken this as a flattering reference to his natural endowments; at all events, he asked, "What if I should give you your life?", and Blood answered promptly, with the correct expression of deep humility, "I would endeavour to deserve it, sire!"

Blood was not only pardoned – to the disgust of Lord Ormonde – but granted Irish lands worth £500 a year. With his pockmarked face, short legs and little blue eyes, he soon became a familiar figure around central London, and made frequent appearances at court.

Talbot Edwards, who recovered, was also rewarded by the king, and achieved his own kind of celebrity as the man who had been robbed of the crown by Colonel Blood. He lived to a ripe old age, always delighted to tell the story to visitors.

Blood's downfall came eight years later, when, in 1679, he quarrelled with his former patron, the scheming Duke of Buckingham. Somehow, perhaps when drunk, Blood came to accuse Buckingham of "gross immorality". Buckingham sued him for £10,000 – which would have ruined Blood – and, to Blood's dismay, he was found guilty. But immediately after the verdict, Blood fell ill, and died on 24 August 1680, at the age of sixty-two.

Even death was quite not the end of the story. There was soon a rumour that Blood had arranged his own "death" to escape paying the fine, and that the coffin contained some other body. The coffin was dug up in the presence of the coroner; when the body had been identified at an inquest it was reburied – a disappointment to his enemies, who still hoped to see him hanged.

Farmer Porter and the Robbers

Nowadays, even in countries with a high crime rate, the countryside is at least safer than the town. In eighteenth century England, it was just as bad.

In the summer of 1751, a farmer named Porter, who lived near Pulford, in Cheshire, engaged some Irish labourers to help with the harvest. One August evening, there was a crash at the door as someone tried to force his way in; the farmer evidently kept it locked as a precaution. Five Irishmen smashed their way into the house, grabbed the farmer and his wife – who were sitting at supper – and tied them up. Porter was ordered to reveal the whereabouts of his cash box, and tried delaying tactics; at this the gang threatened to torture them both. A daughter who had been listening outside the door now rushed into the room, flung herself on her knees, and begged for her father's life; she was also tied up and threatened. She gave way, and told the gang where the valuables were kept.

The youngest daughter, a girl of thirteen, had hidden herself; now she escaped out of the rear door, tiptoed to the stable, led out a horse and rode across the fields to the village. She went to the house of her brother and told him what was happening. The brother and a friend armed themselves – probably with knives and hatchets – and hurried to the farm. A man was on watch; they managed to approach so quietly that he was taken unawares, and promptly killed him. Then they rushed into the parlour, and found the four men holding the farmer – who was naked – and trying to force him to sit on the fire to reveal where he kept his savings. One robber was promptly knocked senseless; the other three fled through the window. The rescuers organized a pursuit, and caught up with two of the robbers on Chester bridge; another man, the ringleader, was caught on a ship at Liverpool. All four men were tried and sentenced to death, but the sentence of the youngest was commuted to transportation for life. The ringleader, Stanley, managed to escape on the eve of his execution. On 25 May 1752, the other two – named M'Canelly and Morgan – were hanged, "their behaviour [being] as decent as could be expected from people of their station".

This kind of house storming was commonplace during the crime wave of the eighteenth century. The robbers organized themselves like military units. A house that was to be attacked was watched for days until the gang knew when they could burst in, and when they were likeliest to be safe from interruption. Stealth and skill were unnecessary in the actual operation; it was conducted like a siege of a town. The M'Canelly and Morgan case shows that the burglars of the mid-eighteenth century had already discovered a method of torture that became common in France at the time of the Revolution, when the robbers were known as *chauffeurs* – warmers. (Professional drivers were later called chauffeurs because the earliest cars were steam driven, so that the driver was literally a stoker, or "fireman".) We have seen that the streets of London were unsafe even by day; footpads operated openly in all the parks and open spaces, while highwaymen waited in every wood and thicket along every main road.

And what were the police doing while all this was going on? The answer is that there were no police. In the countries of Europe, the army kept some kind of order – that is why French policemen were later calls *gens d'armes* or gendarmes – men at arms. But England had no standing army, for it had not been invaded since William the Conqueror. And the British were deeply suspicious of the idea of a police force, believing it would erode their freedom. So in villages, there were local watchmen, and a parish constable – who was a local tradesman who did the job in his spare time. And, as Patrick Pringle points out in his introduction to Goddard's *Memoirs of a Bow Street Runner*, this system worked well enough in the country, but tended to break down in large towns. If a citizen was robbed, he himself had to pursue the robber, setting up a "hue and cry", and if he caught him, had to prosecute him at his own expense. The government tried to make up for the lack of law and order by the barbarity of punishments, so that as many as a dozen men at a time might be hanged at Tyburn (and on several occasions, as many as twenty). The *Gentleman's Magazine* for 1750 recorded: "Executed at Tyburn, July 6, Elizabeth Banks, for stripping a child; Catherine Conway, for forging a seaman's ticket; and Margaret Harvey for robbing her master. They were all drunk." As late as 1801, a boy of thirteen was hanged for breaking into a house and stealing a spoon; two sisters, aged eight and eleven, were hanged at Lynn in 1808. In 1831, a boy of nine was hanged for setting fire to a house, and two years later, another boy of nine was hanged for pushing a stick through a cracked shop window and stealing two pennyworth of printer's colour.

When better-off people left London in the mid-eighteenth century to go to the country, they locked up their houses and took their valuables with them, for they expected the houses to be broken into and robbed. And when someone wanted to recover stolen property, they went along to some dubious characters who knew the underworld, and offered a reward. In the previous century, a retired highwaywoman named Mary Frith, or Moll Cutpurse, set up a shop in Fleet Street to sell the goods stolen by her gang of pickpockets, and her best customers were the victims themselves; she was so successful that she drove every other fence out of the business. Moll died, rich and respected, in 1659, in her mid-seventies. A century later, Jonathan Wild set himself up in the same business, and soon achieved a success far beyond that of Moll Cutpurse. He became a kind of eighteenth century Al Capone, who divided London into districts, with a gang to each; any thief or highwayman who preferred to operate alone was hunted down and hanged on evidence supplied by Wild. He owned a London house and a country mansion, as well as a ship for taking stolen goods overseas; at one point, he even had the effrontery to ask the Mayor of London for freedom of the city in consideration of his great public services. When a law was passed making it illegal to take money for restoring stolen goods to their owners, he found ways around it, and became richer than ever. Eventually, the law caught up with him, and he was hanged in 1725. And within a year or so, London was in the grip of a crime wave that made it dangerous to walk in Covent Garden in broad daylight.

Gin was not the only cause. Others attributed it to the increasing number of sailors who flooded into London as Britain's trade with the rest of the world increased. But the novelist Henry Fielding came closest to the heart of the matter in a pamphlet enquiring into "the late increase of robbers" when he blamed "the vast torrent of luxury which of late years hath poured itself into this nation". England was becoming the richest country in the world, but its wealth existed side by side with appalling poverty. Naturally, the poor tried to divert a little of the wealth into their own pockets. The same thing had happened in ancient Rome and every other civilization that achieved wealth and success . . .

London went on a crime rampage, and it was not confined to the poor. The Mohocks, a society whose members were dedicated to the ambition of "doing all possible hurt to their fellow creatures", were mostly gentlemen. They employed their ample leisure in forcing prostitutes and old women to stand on their heads in tar barrels so that they could prick their legs with their swords; or in making them jump up and down to avoid the swinging blades; in disfiguring their victims by boring out their eyes or flattening their noses; in waylaying servants and, as in the case of Lady Winchelsea's maid, beating them and slashing their faces. To work themselves up to the necessary pitch of enthusiasm for their ferocious games, they first drank so much that they were "quite beyond the possibility of attending to any notions of reason or humanity". Some of the Mohocks seem to have been members of the Bold Bucks who, apparently, had formally to deny the existence of God and eat every Sunday a dish known as Holy Ghost Pie. The ravages of the Bold Bucks were more specifically sexual than those of the Mohocks and consequently, as it was practically impossible to obtain a conviction for rape and as the age of consent was twelve, they were more openly conducted. An expectation of inviolability was, indeed, shared by many, if not most young men of this class. One evening in the 1720s, Richard Savage, who claimed to be a son of the Countess of Macclesfield, quarrelled with some people playing cards in Robinson's coffee-house, lost his temper, and ran one of them through with his sword. He was tried for murder but he was subsequently pardoned. And when a young gentleman named Plunket called at a shop to collect a wig he had ordered he did not hesitate to pick up a razor from the counter and slit the wig-maker's throat from ear to ear, because he would not reduce the price by more than one guinea. Senseless murders such as this were as common as riots . . .

Things began to change for the better in 1729 when a half-pay captain named Thomas De Veil was appointed magistrate for Westminster and Middlesex. A decade earlier, De Veil had been well on the road to ruination with his taste for wine, women and song, which ran him up enormous debts. But he had the sense to retire to a country village and live cheaply before returning to London and setting up as a kind of scrivener, drafting petitions to the government. De Veil made no secret of the fact that he accepted his post as a magistrate because it offered him the opportunity to take bribes and indulge his immense sexual appetite with young ladies who had no other means to bribe him. He had twenty-five legitimate children and an unknown number of bastards, and next door to his office he kept a private room to which he could quickly retire with any attractive woman who appeared before him and was willing to buy her freedom on the couch. But in spite of being virtually a sex maniac, De Veil was also an efficient and hard-working magistrate. Ten years after the execution of Jonathan Wild, one

of London's largest and most desperate robber gangs decided
to kill him when they heard that he was collecting evidence
against them, and well-armed groups of them waited for night
after night around Leicester Fields (the present Leicester
Square), where De Veil had his office. De Veil seems to have
got wind of the plot, and all the waiting finally preyed on the
nerves of one of the thugs, who secretly betrayed his companions to the magistrate. So one of London's most dangerous
gangs was broken up.

De Veil's greatest triumphs came after he transferred his
office to a house in Bow Street, in 1739. Already in his mid-
fifties (and therefore, in eighteenth-century terms, an old man),
De Veil began to build up a reputation as a detective. When an
eating house in Chancery Lane was burgled, he found himself
interrogating a suspect who professed total innocence of the
crime. On a "hunch", De Veil asked the man casually for a loan
of his knife, and he noted that the suspect's pocket knife had a
missing point. He sent a constable round to the eating house
with instructions to look in the lock; the missing point was
found there, and the man convicted. As with most good
detectives, De Veil's success rested upon this keen instinct
about criminal behaviour.

After the death of De Veil in 1746, his position and his house
in Bow Street were taken over by the novelist and playwright
Henry Fielding, who had made the discovery that literature
and poverty are almost synonymous. Fielding had made a
living as a political playwright, until the Prime Minister, Sir
Robert Walpole, grew tired of being satirized, and introduced a
bill that required every play to be licensed by an official called
the Lord Chamberlain – an office that aroused the fury of
generations of playwrights until it was abolished in 1968. That
put an end to Fielding's career as a dramatist, and novels like
Joseph Andrews and *Jonathan Wild* failed to make up for the loss
of income. So, with some reluctance, Fielding decided to accept
the post of Justice of the Peace. His enemies set up a chorus of
derision about the idealistic playwright who had become a
"trading justice". But Fielding had no intention of lining his
own pocket. In his few brief years of office (he was already ill in
1748, and died six years later) he became the most formidable
enemy of crime that London had ever known.

His problem was simple: for every thief and highwayman
who was sent to jail, there were a hundred more left on the
street. With no police force except part-time parish constables,

the London criminal had never known any organized opposition. Yet De Veil had shown that gangs could be destroyed by a determined magistrate. With half a dozen public-spirited friends, Fielding began to organize a group of "thief takers", all ex-parish constables who knew the villains by sight. To us, the system sounds hopelessly amateurish. Victims of robberies were urged to hurry to Fielding's house in Bow Street, whereupon the thief takers would set out in hot pursuit – which is why they soon became known as the Bow Street Runners. And since London's robbers were accustomed to immunity, and seldom bothered to leave their habitual haunts, they were captured in droves. Fielding described his satisfaction as he read the London newspapers, and saw reports of robberies diminishing day by day, until eventually they ceased altogether. He had been granted £600 by the government, and in putting a stop to London's crime wave, he used only half of it.

The next problem was the number of highwaymen and burglars who infested the roads around London. Again, it proved unexpectedly easy to solve. As soon as a few heavily armed constables patrolled the roads, the thieves became nervous, and moved elsewhere. One highwayman had become so accustomed to immunity that he returned regularly to rob the same coach just outside London. Finally, the coachman took a Bow Street Runner with him and when the robber rode up waving his pistol, the Runner fired and blew away half his jaw. The highwayman also fired, but missed; he was taken off to hospital, and thence to jail. This episode took place under the magistracy of Fielding's blind brother John, who continued to be the scourge of London's underworld for more than a quarter of a century after the novelist's death.

The Great Vidocq

At the age of 34, Eugène-François Vidocq was a short, powerfully built man with a scarred face and a jaw like a lion. Born in Arras on 24 July 1775, he had been in trouble most of his life; never serious trouble, but Vidocq had a quick temper and a powerful will, qualities that had led to a number of personal combats and jail sentences. Injustice enraged him, and his attempts to escape from jail had been determined and desperate. By 1808, when he found himself in Paris, the list of his offences was enough to ensure a lifetime in the galleys. He asked to see M. Henry, head of the criminal department of the Paris police, and made him an offer. If he could be guaranteed immunity, he would act as informer against a number of men that the police wanted far more than they wanted Vidocq.

Henry knew he had a bargain, but he felt it could be improved. He allowed Vidocq to go. And when, a few weeks later, Vidocq was denounced by criminal associates and appeared again in front of the chief of police, M. Henry drove a very hard bargain indeed. Vidocq was to become a police spy in one of Paris's toughest prisons, the Bicêtre. If Vidocq was even suspected of being a police informer, he would be found dead the next morning. But, as M. Henry knew, he had no alternative.

Vidocq's task was to obtain evidence against a burglar named Barthélemy Lacour, known to the police as Coco. He had stolen a quantity of silver from a police official. Now he was about to come up for trial, and the police had no evidence. Vidocq's task was to obtain that evidence.

It proved unexpectedly easy. Because of his reputation as an escaper, Vidocq was something of a hero to the other prisoners, and soon became a kind of unofficial lawgiver. One of the first "cases" brought before him in this capacity was, oddly enough, Coco himself, who was suspected of being a police informer. Vidocq saved Coco's life, and so became his trusted intimate. And soon Coco had confided in him that the police would never convict him, for the only witness was a street porter whom the police had failed to question. Coco did not tell Vidocq the porter's name, but he mentioned the street he lived in. Vidocq passed on this information to Henry, and the man was soon traced. Coco never knew how they obtained the evidence that convicted him . . .

For the next two years, Vidocq continued his career of betrayal. Then Henry kept his side of the bargain and allowed him to "escape" on his way to court – the other prisoners were delighted with Vidocq's latest exploit. After that, the great escaper apparently returned to his old habits, spending his days in low wine shops. But the criminals were baffled that the police seemed to know of their best laid plans in advance. No one suspected that the culprit might be the great escaper.

In due course, Vidocq's successes became so great that, in 1810, he was given his own police department; it was called the Sûreté. His priority was to establish a network of informers or "grasses" – a method most police forces now take for granted, but which was established by Vidocq. And from 1810 until he retired in 1833, he scored a remarkable series of successes.

One example will suffice to illustrate his methods. In 1821, a butcher named Fontaine stopped at a roadside inn, and fell into conversation with two respectable-looking travellers; the butcher was delighted when they said they were on their way to a fair at Corbeil, and asked if he could join them. He was carrying a large sum of money, and was worried about robbers. At a lonely spot a few miles further on, they beat him unconscious, stabbed him, and took his money, leaving him for dead. But the butcher survived, and was able to describe his assailants. At the scene of the crime, the police found a fragment of an envelope with part of an address, including "M. Raoul" and "Roche . . ." Vidocq knew a M. Raoul who kept a bar at the Barrière Rochechouart, and whose reputation was sinister.

The butcher had succeeded in delivering a powerful kick at the knee of one of the men, so Vidocq assumed he was looking for a man with a limp. His men kept the bar under surveillance, and soon observed a man with a limp who fitted the butcher's description of one of the robbers. When Vidocq saw him, he recognized a criminal named Court, whom he had arrested some time before for armed robbery. At dawn the next morning he went to Court's room. He told Court he had been accused of smuggling, and observed the expression of relief that crossed the robber's face. Court invited him to search the room, and Vidocq took possession of some weapons, then took Court to the nearest gendarme post.

Now Vidocq used the same technique on Raoul. He explained that Raoul had been denounced for holding anti-Government meetings and distributing seditious pamphlets. Raoul invited him to search the place. There was, as Vidocq expected, nothing. But Raoul had another apartment in Paris. And there, in a bureau, Vidocq found the other half of the envelope. He arrested Raoul and lodged him in prison.

Vidocq proceeded to question Court, carefully failing to mention the attack on the butcher; eventually, Court divulged that he had been concerned in the murder of a poultry dealer,

who had been robbed of four louis. Now, at last, Vidocq
revealed that the crime he was investigating was the attempted murder of the butcher. By now demoralized, Court
also confessed to this, but accused Raoul of the stabbing. Faced
with his confederate's admissions, Raoul also confessed. Both
men were condemned to the guillotine. Yet it is typical of the
close relationship that Vidocq was able to form with criminals
that he went to enormous lengths to make their last days
comfortable, and that when they knelt at the block, they
regarded Vidocq as a friend.

At the age of fifty-eight, Vidocq declined to retire into civilian
life, and became the first private detective in Europe. He wrote
his memoirs, and became a close friend of the novelist Balzac,
who immortalized Vidocq as the sinister but extraordinary
criminal Vautrin; in return, Balzac helped Vidocq to write
novels based on his early life.

chapter two

THE WILD WEST

The First Private Eye

The American equivalent of the great Vidocq was a Scottish-born detective named Allan Pinkerton. Like Vidocq, Pinkerton retired from the official police force to become a private detective, one of the first "private eyes" in the business. (In fact, the term private eye is probably derived from the Pinkerton symbol – an open eye bearing the legend "We never sleep".) But in the second half of the nineteenth century, the Pinkerton detective agency developed an efficiency that surpassed that of Scotland Yard or the Sûreté.

Allan Pinkerton was a radical, who fled from Scotland at the age of twenty-three – in 1842 – to avoid arrest. Working as a cooper in Dundee, Kane County, Illinois, he became an ardent advocate of the abolition of slavery, and helped to smuggle runaway slaves over the border into Canada. And in 1846, chance introduced him to his true vocation: detection. Walking in the woods on an island, he found the remains of a camp fire and trails in the long grass. Many men would have minded their own business; but Pinkerton had a social conscience. The local sheriff accompanied him back to the island, and decided that the camp belonged to a gang of counterfeiters. With Pinkerton's enthusiastic help, he uncovered a cache of fake money and arrested the gang. Only one of them escaped, and

Pinkerton, flushed with triumph, offered to help run him down. He tracked the man, pretended to be a fellow crook, and succeeded in getting him arrested. The result was an overnight reputation as a detective.

On Lake Michigan, not far from Dundee, there was a new city called Chicago – although this little collection of wooden cottages and rooming-houses, with a population of 4,000, was hardly more than a town. Soon after his triumph with the counterfeiters, Pinkerton was asked to become a deputy in Kane County and Cook County, which included Chicago. Like Vidocq, he proved to be a born detective, with a phenomenal memory for faces and a sure instinct for the ways of criminals. But the Chicago police were poorly paid, and when the Post Office engaged Pinkerton as a special agent, he saw that there was more money in private work. This is why, in 1850, he founded the Pinkerton detective agency.

This new, fast-expanding America needed efficient detectives. A fast-growing economy needs to transfer large amounts of money and valuables, and in the wide empty spaces, coaches and railway trains were a great temptation to bandits. The railway came to Chicago in 1852, and the new crime of rail theft

Nickel-plated Smith & Weston, used by Robert Ford to kill Jesse James

was soon costing the express companies and their customers enormous sums of money. In this vast country, Pinkerton often had to behave more like an Indian tracker than a policeman. In 1858, he was summoned to New Haven, where robbers had forced open the Adams Express car and prised open the safes with crow-bars, taking $70,000 in cash and jewellery. Near Stamford, Connecticut, Pinkerton found a bag containing $5,000, and knew he was on the right track. At Norwalk he heard of three men who had tried to hire a buggy, and tracked them down to a house where they had stayed overnight. When he learned that their host had been seen the next day on a train, carrying a heavy package that evidently made him nervous, he guessed that it contained the rest of the loot. He tracked the man to New York, but found that he had already left for Canada – but without the package. And under his questioning, the man's niece led him to the money and jewellery, hidden in the cellar. The gang was arrested, and Pinkerton completed the job by arresting the leader in Canada.

The Drysdale Bank Robbery

One early case from the Pinkerton archives is so incredible that it sounds like fiction. In 1855, a young bank teller named George Gordon was murdered late at night when working in his office; he was the nephew of the bank president. The bank vault was open, and $130,000 was missing. Gordon had been killed by a hammer blow dealt from the left. In the fireplace there were remains of burnt papers and clothing – the murderer had stayed on to burn his bloodstained coat. The only clues were two pieces of paper – a bloodstained page containing some pencilled figures – found under the body – and a partly burnt fragment of paper that had been twisted into a "spill" to light the fire. When Pinkerton unfolded this, he found that it was a note for $927.78, and that it was signed Alexander P. Drysdale, the county clerk, a man of unimpeachable reputation. The bloodstained page contained a subtraction sum – $1,252 minus $324.22 – the result being $927.78.

Pinkerton asked to see the bank balances of a number of

prominent local businessmen whom Gordon might have admitted to the bank after hours. Drysdale's account showed a figure of $324.22. Now Pinkerton was able to reconstruct the crime. Drysdale had come to the bank in the evening to request a loan of $1,252. Gordon had agreed – but had subtracted from this sum the amount already in Drysdale's account. Then he had opened the vault. Overcome by sudden temptation, Drysdale had seized a hammer someone had left in the office and killed his friend.

Pinkerton was certain that Drysdale was the killer, but how to prove it? He began by finding an excuse to get Drysdale to write something, and noted that he was left-handed, like the killer. Next, he sent for three of his operatives from Chicago – an older man, a woman, and a young man called Green. They posed as visitors to the town, and began secretly investigating Drysdale's affairs. Green, a good carpenter, found himself a job in the local carpenter's shop, where all the old men gathered in the evening to gossip. The older detective, who was calling

---

The most famous siege in criminal history began with a robbery that went wrong.

On the freezing, windy night of 16 December 1910, a man who lived next to a jeweller's shop in Houndsditch, East London, heard the noise of hammering. Suspecting – correctly – that robbers were trying to break through the wall into the jewellers, he called the police. P.C. Piper knocked on the door of 11 Exchange Buildings and asked if the "missus" was there. A foreigner told him she was out and he said he would call back. Piper returned with several more policemen – all unarmed – and knocked again. This time they were admitted, but as soon as they were inside, shooting began. One policeman was killed outright, two fatally injured, and four more wounded. Outside, a policeman grabbed the gang leader, George Gardstein; another member of the gang fired at the policeman, and hit Gardstein instead. They hurried away, supporting Gardstein, who was bleeding to death. Gardstein died that night at a nearby house – rented by a Russian anarchist named Friz Svaars – at 59 Grove Street.

The doctor who had been called to attend Gardstein notified the police, who found the body of Gardstein in the bed. Only one member of the gang, a little hunchback named Sara Trassjonsky, was still there, frantically burning papers. Her lover Peter Piatkow himself Andrews, learned by chance one day that young Green bore a close resemblance to the dead George Gordon. And when Pinkerton learned of this, he formulated an incredible plan. Not far from Drysdale's home was a spot known as Rocky Creek, reputed to be haunted. "Andrews", pretending to be interested in a local plot of land, got Drysdale to take him through Rocky Creek at dusk, and as they rode among the trees, a ghostly figure walked across the path, its hair matted with blood. Drysdale shrieked; Andrews looked astonished and insisted that he could see nothing.

The woman operative had succeeded in getting herself invited into Drysdale's home as a guest of Mrs Drysdale, and she observed that her host was beginning to suffer nightmares and was prone to sleep-walking. Green, dressed as the ghost, kept up the pressure by occasionally flitting about outside the house when Drysdale was wandering around restlessly. Finally, Pinkerton appeared and arrested Drysdale, who protested his innocence. They took him to the

---

– who became known as Peter the Painter because he painted scenery for anarchist plays at a nearby club – had already escaped.

During the next month, a nationwide manhunt led to the arrest of eight gang members, including two women. On 2 January 1911, police received information that two more – Fritz Svaars and a man named Josef – were in the second floor room of Mrs Betsy Gershon at 100 Sidney Street. In fact, Mrs Gershon was a prisoner, and the men had taken her skirt and shoes to prevent her from going out. The police surrounded the house and evacuated the other floors. Early the next day they sent the landlady to go and ask Mrs Gershon to go and fetch a doctor, and the anarchists allowed her to go.

At dawn the police threw gravel at the window, and the anarchists opened fire. From the Tower of London the Scots Guards were sent, and the Home Secretary, Winston Churchill, arrived to watch the siege. The firing continued all morning. At one o'clock the house burst into flames, and the police refused to let firemen near it. One fireman was fatally injured as the house collapsed. The bodies of the two anarchists were found in the charred ruins, one shot in the head.

Peter the Painter was never caught, and is said to have died in America in 1914.

bank, and when the "ghost" appeared from behind the teller's counter, Drysdale fainted. When he recovered, he still continued to protest his innocence, and it began to look as if Pinkerton's bold strategy had failed. But when Drysdale was shown the two scraps of paper proving his involvement, he broke down and confessed. The stolen money was found hidden in a creek near his home.

The Reno Gang

But most of Pinkerton's early cases demanded persistence and courage rather than this kind of ingenuity. His most remarkable feat of the 1860s was undoubtedly his break-up of the Reno gang, America's first gang of organized outlaws. The five brothers – Frank, John, Simeon, Clinton, and William – were the sons of an Indiana farmer who lived at Seymour, Indiana. John left home at sixteen – in 1855 – and spent some time wandering around Mississippi, working on steamboats and learning to make a living by his wits. Back home, he propounded a scheme of amazing simplicity. The nearby small town of Rockford was prosperous and virtually unprotected. A series of arson attacks so terrified the inhabitants that they began moving elsewhere. Then the Renos bought most of Rockford at bargain prices.

During the Civil War, the Reno brothers served in the army; but most of them soon deserted. During the war, the bloodthirsty southerner William Clarke Quantrill led a band of guerrillas who were little more than robbers and murderers – it included Jesse James, "Bloody Bill" Anderson, and Cole Younger – and although most of the gang was wiped out in 1865, James and Cole Younger went on to become wandering outlaws. Meanwhile, back in Seymour, the Reno brothers formed their own outlaw gang, specializing in robbing county treasury offices. And in 1866, they invented a new crime – holding up trains. They boarded the wood-burning Ohio and Mississippi railroad coach as ordinary passengers at Seymour, then strolled down to the Adams Express car, forced the door, and held up the messenger at gunpoint. They pulled the communication cord, stopping the train, and rolled the safe off it. But they were still trying to burst it open in the woods when a posse drove them to abandon it. Nevertheless, John Reno had succeeded in seizing $10,000 in notes.

Pinkerton was asked to take on the case. The bandits had worn masks, but he had no doubt they were the Renos. A few weeks later, a new saloon was opened in Seymour – the amiable, round-faced man who ran it was really a Pinkerton operative called Dick Winscott – and the Renos soon became customers. Winscott even succeeded in persuading the brothers to allow him to take a group photograph – possibly the first time photography was used in crime detection. (Pinkerton had copies made and circulated.)

Seymour was an armed camp run by outlaws, and there was no chance of arresting the Renos on the spot. Allan Pinkerton enlisted the aid of Dick Winscott. The Renos were being sought for a bank robbery in Gallatin, Missouri, and had been identified by witnesses through their photographs. One afternoon soon after, the train stopped in Seymour, and Allan Pinkerton looked cautiously out of the window. On the platform he recognized the jovial figure of Dick Winscott, talking to John

Jesse James

Reno. Six muscular men, accompanied by a sheriff from Cincinnati – another city that held warrants for the Renos – strolled casually off the train, surrounded John Reno, and hustled him aboard. Reno bellowed for help, but although the other Reno brothers commandeered another train and pursued the kidnappers, John Reno was handed over to the Gallatin authorities and sentenced to twenty-five years in jail.

In February 1868, Frank Reno – now the gang leader – led a raid on the Harrison County treasury at Magnolia, Iowa, which netted $14,000. Using his skills as a tracker, Pinkerton found them hiding in the home of a pillar of the Methodist church in Council Bluffs, and arrested them in a sudden raid. But the jail in Council Bluffs was not strong enough to hold them, and when the sheriff arrived the next morning he found the cells empty and a chalked inscription: "April Fool" – the date being 1 April 1868.

Local citizens were becoming enraged at the impunity the gang seemed to enjoy. The Reno brothers were not the kind of jolly outlaws who became folk heroes; they were bullies and killers. In desperation, some of the bolder Seymour residents formed a Vigilance Committee. The Renos heard the rumours, and made bloodthirsty threats.

After a train robbery at Marshfield, Indiana, which netted the gang $96,000, Pinkerton decided they had to be caught by cunning. He circulated rumours that $100,000 in gold was to be shipped via Seymour. The train's engineer pretended to agree to co-operate with the gang and tipped off Pinkerton exactly where the robbery would take place. And as the outlaws stopped the train and burst open the Express car, they were met by a volley of shots from Pinkerton's men. Most of the gang escaped, but the next day, three of them were captured in a thicket and arrested. But one dark night a few weeks later, the train on which they were being sent to their trial was stopped by men waving red lanterns; the three bandits were dragged off the train and lynched. A few weeks later, another three bandits who had been tracked down by Pinkerton were intercepted on their way to jail by a mob and lynched. The Reno gang left in Seymour began to fight back; members of the Vigilance Committee had rocks thrown through their windows; there were night raids, beatings, and mutilations. When Simeon and William Reno were arrested by Pinkerton detectives in Indianapolis, Vigilance Committee members received messages: "If the Renos are lynched, you die." The Vigilance Committee decided that if the Renos were not lynched, things would remain as bad as ever. The authorities decided to transfer the two Renos to the more secure New Albany jail. On 6 September 1868, there was a determined attempt by vigilantes to break into the Lexington jail, but the Renos had already been moved. They were joined in New Albany by their brother Frank, who had been arrested in Canada, together with a gang member named Charles Anderson. But on 11 December vigilantes surrounded the jail and burst their way in with a battering ram. The sheriff was beaten unconscious, and his keys taken. Then the Reno brothers and Anderson were dragged from their cells and lynched. As the vigilantes dispersed, prisoners watched from their cells and saw Simeon gasping for breath on the end of his rope; it took half an hour before he ceased to struggle.

The Vigilance Committee issued a notice, naming other members of the gang still in Seymour – including brother Clinton – and declaring that if they wished to remain as honest citizens, they would be welcome; otherwise they would meet the fate of the others. The gang accepted the ultimatum sullenly, and the outlaws ceased to be a power in Indiana.

Jesse James

Pinkerton was altogether less successful in his attempts to catch Jesse James. Like the Reno brothers, Jesse and his brother Frank came back from the Civil War, in which they fought for the South, wondering whether the methods of Quantrill's guerrillas could not be applied with equal success in peacetime. On 13 February 1866, ten men rode into Liberty, Missouri, and robbed the bank; on their way out of town, one of them shot down an unarmed student on his way to college, then, whooping and firing pistols, the gang rode out of town. It was the first of many pointless murders committed by the gang led by this modern "Robin Hood". In December 1869, the James gang robbed the same bank in Gallatin, Missouri, that the Reno brothers had robbed two years earlier, and James shot the manager in cold blood.

The Pinkertons began trailing the James gang at about this time, but had no success. In February 1874, a Pinkerton operative, John W. Whicher, succeeded in infiltrating the gang, but was recognized and murdered. On 6 January 1875, the Pinkertons received a tip-off that Jesse was visiting his mother, Mrs Zerelda Samuel; they surrounded the house and tossed in a "smoke bomb". It killed James's eight-year-old half-brother, and blew off his mother's arm. The incident brought much sympathy for the James brothers and indignant criticism of the brutality of Pinkerton. Jesse James was so angry that he spent four months in Chicago trying to get Pinkerton alone so he could kill him; he was unsuccessful.

On 7 August 1876, an attempt to rob the bank in Northfield,

Edward "Ned" Kelly is remembered as an outlaw in the same tradition as Robin Hood, a national hero who stole as a protest against authority. He was the son of a man transported to Tasmania from Belfast in 1841, and he himself began his criminal career early. He stole cattle and horses, and while still in his mid-teens he served a three year prison sentence.

His criminal career really took flight when in April 1878, he wounded a police officer who had come to the family home in Victoria to arrest his brother, also on a charge of rustling. As a result, the warrant was extended to cover the both of them and they took to the bush to hide out and plan. While they were away, the remaining portion of their family were arrested, tried and imprisoned for theft and resisting.

The two Kellys joined up with two other criminals, Steve Hart and Joe Byrne, and as the Kelly Gang, terrorized the local area, avoiding capture through a network of sympathizers and informants that hated the police. The gang's robbery technique often involved rounding up most of the inhabitants of a town and holding them prisoner in the local hotel while they stole anything worthwhile that they could find. The gang had no reservations about killing any policemen that got near them.

Even after the police had arrested many sympathizers under the Apprehension of Felons Act, the gang continued to evade them. The officers did not dare arrest any women, for fear of the public outcry that this would cause, yet a large proportion of the gang's "Bush telegraph" consisted of female sympathizers and

Minnesota, went disastrously wrong; the citizens all rushed outdoors with guns, and most of the bandits were either killed or wounded; James's cousin Cole Younger and his brother Bob were captured soon after and sentenced to life imprisonment. James formed a second gang, but it never met with the same success as the earlier one. On 7 August 1881, the gang committed its last train robbery, netting only $1,500. Harassment by the Pinkertons was breaking their nerve. On 3 April 1882, Jesse James was planning another robbery with two new gang members, Bob and Charlie Ford, when Bob Ford pulled out his gun and shot James in the back. He had agreed to deliver Jesse James to the state governor for reward money and amnesty. The murder of Jesse James – at the age of 34 – made

thus remained intact. As the robberies continued the police were heavily criticized in all quarters.

Meanwhile the Kelly gang were planning an ambush in which they hoped to kill many officers. A former accomplice called Sherritt was being held under police protection. As a means to attract the police, Joe Byrne shot Sherritt dead, while the rest of the gang forced two railwaymen to sabotage the track outside town. The plan was to let the train carrying the officers de-rail, and then kill them while they were still confused and wounded. As usual the gang held the local population in a hotel, but a schoolteacher succeeded in evading them and warning the police. Soon they arrived in town by different means and surrounded the hotel.

Realizing that the situation was hopeless, Dan Kelly and Steve Hart took poison and died. Joe Byrne was shot dead by the police. Ned Kelly, determined to escape the police that he hated so much, made a break for the bush and, although wounded, succeeded in making a makeshift suit of armour out of plough mouldboards. Wearing this as protection, Kelly tried to break through the police line. He was brought down by bullet wounds to his legs, but not until he had withstood twenty-five hits on the armour.

Kelly was tried in Melbourne in 1880, and was hanged on November 11. The repeated failures of the police prompted an inquiry by the Royal Commission. Kelly still remains a hero for anti-authoritarians everywhere; at his trial he was described as a quiet, self-possessed man with a fanatical hatred of the police.

him more of a folk hero than ever, and his brother Frank was acquitted several times of crimes he had obviously committed (he died of old age in 1915). Allan Pinkerton died two years after Jesse James, at the age of sixty-five but the agency continued with unabated success under sons and grandsons.

The Dalton Gang

One of the great early classics of American crime is Thomas S. Duke's *Celebrated Criminal Cases of America*, published in 1910. Duke was a captain in the San Francisco Police Force, and his style is often rough and ready; nevertheless, it has a dramatic feeling of immediacy. Here is Duke's account of the Dalton gang.

After the extermination of the James–Younger gang, the Dalton brothers stepped in and occupied the place once filled by them in the ranks of bloodthirsty criminals. In the Dalton family were six boys, named Ben, Frank, Grattan, William, Robert and Emmet.

In April, 1889, the Territory of Oklahoma was thrown open. For weeks previous to that time, thousands of people were camped along the frontier so as to be located in the most advantageous position to rush in at the appointed time and stake claims on the most valuable land, which they afterwards purchased from the Government for less than two dollars per acre.

For many months after the rush, lawlessness reigned supreme in this Territory. Bob Dalton was performing the duties of a Deputy United States Marshal at this time, but he began to associate with the outlaws and finally became a leader among them. Emmet and Grattan joined the gang, but in 1890 the Territory became "too warm" for the Daltons, so they went to California, where their brother Bill had rented a ranch in Tulare County.

At 7:50 pm, January 6, 1891, train No. 17 left Alila, Cal., for Bakersfield, but had scarcely gone one mile on its journey when Engineer Thorn and Fireman Radliff were confronted by two masked men who stood on the tender of the engine. The engineer was ordered to stop the train and the frowning muzzle of a pistol placed against his temple caused an immediate compliance with the command.

The engineer and fireman were then ordered to accompany the robbers to the express car. The express messenger, suspecting what had happened, put out the lights in his car and lay on the floor. He was ordered to open the door, but his reply was a shot from his revolver which was followed by a fusillade, during which Fireman Radliff was mortally wounded. The desperadoes then gave up the struggle and fled. A pursuit was at once begun but all trace of them was lost until 12 March. On this date Sheriff O'Neil of Paso Robles arrested William Dalton on the strength of evidence he had gathered, and upon being interrogated Dalton made some damaging admissions, which led to the arrest of his brother Grattan a few days later.

Both were taken to Visalia and charged with this crime, but William was eventually acquitted. On 7 July Grattan was convicted, after having tried to throw the entire blame on his brothers, Robert and Emmet, who were still at large. His sentence was continued until 6 October, but on Sunday night, September 26, he in some mysterious manner obtained possession of the keys to the prison kitchen and cell door, and in company with one William Smith, a convicted burglar, and W.R. Beck, a notorious character, escaped.

Services were being conducted in a church nearby, and the team belonging to George McKinley, one of the worshippers, stood awaiting him, but the three desperadoes took possession of it and made good their escape.

On December 24, Sheriff Hensly of Fresno met Grattan Dalton in the mountains, and after an exchange of several shots the bandit again escaped. He then joined Emmet and Bob in the Oklahoma reservation.

Deputy United States Marshal Ransom Payne incurred the displeasure of this gang, because he had the "audacity" to attempt to capture them. Bob and Emmet Dalton and one Charlie Bryant learned that this officer would leave Wichita, Okla. Ter., on the evening of May 9, 1891, for his home in Guthrie, so they decided to rob this train and kill the officer. They went to a little station called Wharton and ordered the stationkeeper to signal the train to stop. When the train came to a standstill, one bandit took charge of the engineer and fireman, and the remaining two went through the train inquiring for Payne. That official being alone and not knowing the number of bandits in the party, and realizing that he would probably be killed if the Daltons were in the gang and discovered him, decided to evade them and left the train and hid in the brush near the track.

Failing to locate Payne, the two desperadoes proceeded to the express car, where they obtained about $1,500. The bandits then made their escape on horses, and when the train left Payne came out of hiding and ran to the stationhouse, where he found the stationkeeper bound and gagged. The next day a posse was organized and in August, 1891, Bryant was arrested. One of the posse named Edward Short took charge of him, while the remainder continued in pursuit of the Daltons. Short boarded the train with his prisoner, and when the train stopped at a little station he left Bryant, who was handcuffed, in the charge of Wells-Fargo's agent, to whom he loaned a revolver. The agent, believing the prisoner was asleep, laid the pistol down and continued with his work. Just then Bryant jumped up, seized the weapon and attempted to escape. Short saw him leave the car and instantly drew another revolver. A duel followed with the result that both men were killed.

The Dalton gang remained in seclusion until the night of June 2, 1892, when Bob, Grattan and Emmet Dalton, assisted by three or four others, held up the Atchison, Topeka and Santa Fe train at Red Rock Station, Oklahoma. As the passenger train stopped at this station only when signalled to do so, the stationkeeper was ordered to display the necessary signal. When the train stopped the engineer was overpowered by two robbers and the remainder of the gang proceeded to the express car, where $1,800 was obtained, after which they escaped in the darkness.

In the early part of the following July, the territorial police and railroad officials learned that the Dalton gang were rendezvoused near the Missouri, Kansas and Texas Railroad in Oklahoma, and as they had profited little financially from their recent raids it was suspected that one of the trains on this road would soon be attacked. It was therefore decided to put a heavily armed posse on each train. Thus prepared, the authorities rather welcomed an attack, feeling confident that it would mean the extermination of the gang.

On the evening of July 15, 1892, the three Daltons, reinforced by five others, rode up to Adair station in Indian Territory and after robbing the agent they ordered him to signal the train to stop. Conductor George Scales and Engineer Ewing were immediately taken into custody, and the party then went to the express car which was in charge of Messenger George Williams, who reluctantly opened the safe and several thousand dollars were stolen.

The "guards," who were lounging in the smoker instead of being with the messenger, did not appear very anxious to perform their duty, although some of them ventured out and opened fire in a half-hearted way. A stray bullet struck and mortally wounded a Dr W. Goff, who was at the time in a nearby drug store. Two of the guards named Kinney and La Flore were also shot, but their wounds were superficial. During the fusillade, a wagon was driven up to the train, the bags of money were thrown in and the bandits again escaped.

The next raid attempted by these bandits occurred at their old home in Coffeyvile, Kansas, on October 5, 1892. The gang on this fatal day consisted of Bob, Grattan and Emmet Dalton, Dick Broadwell and Bill Powers. They rode into town about 9:30 am, and were recognized by a merchant named Alexander McKenna, who quickly but quietly rushed about notifying everyone he met.

The five bandits proceeded to C.M. Condon's bank and Grattan Dalton, Powers and Broadwell entered the bank, where they found President Charles Carpenter and Cashier Charles Ball.

As soon as the three men entered this bank, Bob and Emmet Dalton hastened to the First National Bank across the street, as it was planned to rob both institutions simultaneously. In each bank the bandits were informed that the time lock would not be off for several minutes and the robbers decided to wait.

In the meantime the news of the movements of the gang had spread through the town like wildfire, and the gunsmiths were loaning weapons and ammunition to all who desired them. As a result both banks were soon surrounded by determined men, all heavily armed, and the bullets began to fly through the windows of the bank.

When the vault was opened at the First National, Cashier Thomas Ayers handed out the money, amounting to over $20,000. Bob and Emmet Dalton put this in a sack and escaped out of the back entrance. They ran in the direction of Condon's Bank, but when they observed the crowd of armed men in front of that institution, they began firing, with the result that a young clerk named Lucius Baldwin was instantly killed.

In the general battle that followed, two shoemakers, named

George Cubine and Charles Brown, were killed by Bob Dalton when he saw them attempting to shoot him. Immediately after killing these men, Bob saw Cashier Ayers of the bank with his rifle raised, and Dalton shot him in the head, inflicting a serious but not fatal wound.

At this time the three robbers in Condon's Bank rushed out into the shower of bullets with about $3,000, and joining Bob and Emmet Dalton, they ran to their horses, but did not have an opportunity to mount.

John Kloehr, a stableman, and City Marshal Charles Connelly, both armed with rifles, then joined in the battle. Grat Dalton killed Connelly and almost immediately afterwards Kloehr killed Bob Dalton. Bandit Powers was the next to be killed and Grattan Dalton was then killed by Kloehr.

All of the bandits having been killed except Broadwell and Emmet Dalton, these two, realizing the great odds against them, mounted their horses and attempted to escape. They had only gone a short distance, however, when Emmet wheeled about and in the face of a heavy fire, returned to the body of his brother Bob, and as he was in the act of lifting the body with the intention of carrying it away on his horse, a load of buckshot was poured into his back and he fell unconscious.

Broadwell was fatally wounded as he attempted to escape and his body was found a short distance from town. Several horses were also killed and many citizens wounded.

Emmet Dalton finally recovered from what were diagnosed as necessarily fatal wounds, and he was sentenced to serve the remainder of his life at the State Prison at Lansing, but Governor Hock pardoned him in January, 1907.

After the tragic death of his brothers, Bill Dalton reorganized the gang and operations were resumed in Oklahoma Territory. Their rendezvous was in the extreme eastern part of the Cherokee strip, but considerable amount of their time was spent in a little village called Ingalls. As they purchased their provisions, ammunition and whisky in this village, they were shielded by those who profited from their trade.

On September 1, 1893, Bill Dalton, Bill Doolin, Arkansas Tom, George Newton and Tulca Jack were drinking at the bar in the village hotel when the place was surrounded by a posse consisting of ex-Sheriff Hixon, Deputy Marshals Thomas Houston, Lafe Hadley, Dick Speed and several other officials and civilians. The outlaws ran out of the place and at the beginning of the firing Deputy Speed was killed. Hadley killed Dalton's horse and the bandit fell and laid motionless on the ground. Hadley, believing him to be dead, approached, but as he drew near Dalton jumped up and shot the deputy in the head, killing him instantly. The bandit then mounted the murdered officer's horse, and although severely wounded, he escaped.

During the battle Deputy Houston and a clerk named Simmons were also killed, and S.W. Ransom, N.S. Murray and a twelve-year-old boy named Briggs were seriously wounded. All of the bandits escaped with the exception of Arkansas Tom, who was barricaded in the hotel and who subsequently surrendered on the condition that he would be protected from the mob. The next day it was ascertained that none of the bandits escaped without wounds.

The last raid committed by the Dalton gang occurred at the First National Bank at Longview, Texas, at 3 pm, May 23, 1894. At this time two roughly dressed men entered the bank and presented a note to President Clemmons, which read as follows:

"Home, May 23rd.
"This will introduce you to Charles Spreckelmeyers, who wants some money and is going to have it.   B. and F."

When Mr Clemmons read the note and looked up, he was covered by a rifle in the hands of one bandit while the other went behind the counter and secured $2000.00 in ten-dollar bills and nine twenty-dollar bills. City Marshal Muckley immediately learned of the raid and hurriedly gathered a posse who gave the robbers a hot battle. One of the bandits, Geo. Bennett, alias Jim Wallace, was killed as was also George Buckingham of the posse. Marshal Muckley and J.W. McQueen, a saloon-keeper, received serious wounds.

On June 7, 1894, a suspicious looking character, giving the name of Wall, came into the town of Ardmore, I.T., with two women who also acted quite mysteriously. They purchased about $200.00 worth of provisions and then called at the express office. The attention of the authorities was attracted by the peculiar actions of the trio, and while they made many conflicting statements, the information was elicited that they were living near a place called Elk. Sheriff Hart immediately organized a posse as he believed the provisions were purchased for some persons who feared to come to town, and as the Dalton gang was uppermost in his mind, he concluded that these three persons were connected with the gang. They were held prisoners and at 8 am the next morning the house where it was suspected that Dalton was hiding was surrounded.

Dalton came to one of the windows and seeing some of the posse he jumped from a window on the opposite side of the building and started to run.

Sheriff Hart called on him to halt, but as he ignored the command, one shot was fired from the sheriff's rifle and Dalton dropped dead without uttering a word.

The house was then searched and conclusive evidence was obtained, not only as to Dalton's identity, but also that he participated in the Longview bank robbery. The officials then returned to Ardmore and when the mysterious trio were informed of the death of Dalton, one of the women became hysterical and said she was Dalton's wife and that they were married at her home in Merced, California, in 1888.

The D'Autremont Brothers

In the mid-1920s, the most famous American sleuth was a man named Edward Oscar Heinrich, who became known as "the Edison of Crime Detection". Before he became Professor of Criminology at the Berkeley Campus of the University of California, Heinrich had been the city chemist in Tacoma, Washington.

The case that brought him celebrity began on 11 October 1923, when a train bound from Oregon to San Francisco was held up by bandits in the Siskiyou Mountains. The train was crawling through a tunnel when two men dropped off the roof of the engine tender and pointed guns at the engineer and fireman; they were made to stop the train and then marched up a slope at gunpoint and made to stand with raised hands. A third man placed a large package beside the mail car – which was half-way out of the tunnel – and ran. A moment later, there was a violent explosion, which blasted open the car and set it on fire. Then the engineer and fireman were ordered to pull the rest of the train out of the tunnel. This proved to be impossible. The bandits were becoming increasingly panicky, and when the brakeman ran out of the tunnel to see what was happening, one of them raised a shotgun and shot him dead. Then the engineer and fireman were deliberately executed. And the bandits, who realized that they were not going to get into the blazing mail car, disappeared. A mail clerk named Edwin Daugherty was burned to death.

Police from Ashland, Oregon, found a detonating device with batteries near the tunnel. Nearby there was a revolver, a pair of shoes, and a pair of greasy denim overalls.

Posses galloped off in all directions looking for the robbers. Meanwhile, the sheriff examining the detonator wondered whether its batteries might not have come from a nearby garage. He hurried there, and arrested the mechanic he found working in a pair of greasy overalls that looked very similar to those found near the detonator. But the mechanic maintained his innocence, and the police were unable to find the slightest shred of evidence to link him with the crime.

Edward O. Heinrich was obviously the man to approach, and the police sent him the overalls found at the scene of the crime. Within two days he told them over the telephone: "You are holding the wrong man. The grime on these overalls is not car grease. It is fir pitch. In the pocket I found particles of Douglas fir needles. The man who wore these overalls is a left-handed lumberjack. He is between twenty-one and twenty-five years of age, about five feet ten inches tall, and he weighs about 165 lb. His hair is medium light brown, his hands and feet are small, and he is a man of fastidious habits."

Later, Heinrich explained how he had made these deductions. The fir chips were in the right-hand pocket, which meant that the man stood with his right side towards the tree as he was chopping it down; a right-handed man stands with his left side to the tree. Besides, the left-handed pockets were more used than the right, and the overalls were buttoned on the left. The overall bottoms had been folded to fit into boots, and the position of the suspender buckles indicated the height and build of the wearer. A single hair adhering to a button told Heinrich that the man was white – Negro hair or Indian hair is quite different. Nail clippings that had been caught in a front pocket had been cut with a precision that indicated a man of fastidious habits. The size of the shoes had indicated a man with small feet, and it followed that his hands were also small.

Heinrich had found another clue. In the pencil pocket of the overalls he had found a scrap of folded paper that the police had missed. It was a receipt for a registered letter bearing a code number. The Post Office was able to tell the police that it had been issued in Eugene, Oregon, as a receipt for $50 sent by a man called Roy D'Autremont to Ray D'Autremont in Lakewood, New Mexico.

It was easy to locate Paul D'Autremont, the elderly father of the brothers, in Eugene. He told them that his three sons – the twins Roy and Ray, and their brother Hugh – had been missing since the day of the hold-up. And Roy was a left-handed lumberjack.

Heinrich's examination of the gun found near the detonator left no doubt that the D'Autremont brothers were the bandits. A hidden number led the police to the store in Seattle where it had been purchased by a man calling himself William Elliott. Heinrich, who was also a handwriting expert, was able to state that Elliott's handwriting was that of Roy D'Autremont.

Even the reward of $15,000 offered by the railway company failed to produce information of the brothers' whereabouts. But in March 1927, an army sergeant saw a "Wanted" poster, and thought that Hugh D'Autremont resembled a private he had known in the Philippines. Hugh D'Autremont was arrested in Manila. A month later, Roy and Ray were recognized at the steel mill in Steubenville, Ohio, where they were working. All three brothers were sentenced to life imprisonment.

chapter three

VICTORIAN VILLAINIES

The Great Gold-Dust Robbery

Until the end of the eighteenth century, most robbers were clumsy amateurs – footpads, highwaymen and burglars who lived from day to day, and usually ended on the gallows before they reached their thirties. But the Industrial Revolution created new wealth, and brought a new class of criminal: the bold planner who was willing to risk ten years in jail for an ambitious coup that might make him wealthy for life. And the simplest way to go about it was to find some underpaid clerk or warehouseman, and bribe him to take part – what we now call an "inside job".

The first of the great "inside jobs" happened in London Docks in 1839.

On 25 March 1839, two boxes of gold dust addressed to Hartley and Co. arrived at St Katherine's Dock from Brazil. They had just been forwarded from Falmouth by a shipper called Carne and Co. and the contents were worth £4,600. That same morning, Hartley and Co. received a letter from Carne and Co. telling them that the gold-dust was about to arrive, and that it would be collected by a representative of the agents of the Brazilian Mining Company.

Early that afternoon, the man they were expecting arrived to collect the boxes, and produced documents that described them

in detail. A clerk named Lewin Caspar, who was in charge of
the boxes, was heard to mutter that he hoped the papers were
genuine. But he handed over the boxes, and the man drove off
in a cab. Half an hour later, his employers were thrown into
panic when another man arrived from the agents, and demanded the boxes, producing another set of obviously genuine
documents. It seemed that Lewin Caspar had been right, and
the first man was an impostor.

For Hartley and Co. it was a serious blow – they would have
to reimburse the £4,600, enough to threaten them with bank-
ruptcy. The London police force had only been in existence for
ten years, and was not noted for its efficiency. Nevertheless,
two detectives named Lea and Roe were given the task of
tracking down the robber.

They began by tracing the horse-drawn cab in which he had
escaped. The driver said he had been paid off in Wood Street, in
the City, and that the man with the two boxes had then hired
another cab and driven off towards Holborn. The second cabbie
was finally traced, and told them that he had driven the man to
a house in New Street. But the detectives arrived too late; the
man had already left and moved to lodgings in Goodman's
Fields. Now several days behind him, the detectives arrived to
find that he had left this lodging too, this time without leaving
an address. But, to their relief, he proved to be known to his
landlord in Goodman's Fields. He was a married man named
Henry Moss, and he worked as a foreman to a watchmaker in
Goodman's Fields. Mrs Moss's female servant had been left
behind, and told the detectives that on the morning of the
robbery, Moss had left home wearing his best clothes, which
was unusual. He came back to his New Street lodging with two
large boxes. The next morning, the servant had noticed burnt
fragments of these boxes in the grate.

The detectives picked up another important piece of information. Before the robbery, Henry Moss had been seeing a
great deal of a Jewish watchmaker called Ellis Caspar, who had
once been his employer. And Ellis Caspar was the father of
Lewin Caspar, the clerk who had handed over the boxes of gold
dust. This was too much of a coincidence, and both Caspars
were promptly arrested.

While they were still searching for Henry Moss, the police
decided that the next step was to find out what might have
happened to the gold. A check among London's bullion dealers
revealed that Bull and Co. of Cheapside had recently bought a

large quantity of gold bars from a man called Henry Solomon. Solomon, a gold refiner, admitted that he had sold gold bars worth £1,200 to the bullion dealer, but claimed he had made them from melting down gold snuff-boxes. The police did not believe him, and when they told him so, Mr Solomon became sullen and uncooperative. These were the days when London was full of the kind of anti-semitism reflected in Dickens' Fagin – *Oliver Twist* came out the same year – and the *New Newgate Calendar* remarks that the gold-dust robbers "were of the Jewish persuasion, and the proverbial cunning and habits of cheating of these people were exemplified throughout the enquiry". There can be no doubt Mr Solomon's civil rights were violated in the course of his interrogation. Although the evidence against him was non-existent, he appeared before the magistrates, together with the Caspars, charged with receiving the gold dust.

Meanwhile, Henry Moss, who was hiding out in Peckham, had heard of the arrest of the Caspars. It also emerged later that he suspected the Caspars of intending to cheat him. So Moss decided to give himself up and turn police informer. His story was that he had acted in complete innocence. Ellis Caspar had approached him a year ago, and told him that his son Lewin now had a job as a clerk at a shipping agents. He wanted Moss to do him a small favour – take some papers, and go and collect some boxes from Hartley and Co. Moss was assured that he was doing nothing illegal, and agreed. But on this first occasion, something had gone amiss – Caspar said that a ship had failed to arrive. He was given ten shillings, and told they might need his help on some future occasion.

The occasion came a year later, when Henry Moss was finally given the necessary papers, and told to collect two boxes from Lewin Caspar at Hartley and Co. He followed his instructions, and took the boxes back to his lodgings in a cab. When he got there, he found Ellis Caspar waiting in a state of jitters. The police were on the trail, said Mr Caspar, and Moss would have to move the next morning. After this, the boxes were opened, and proved to contain a number of tins. Then the Mosses were told to burn the boxes.

Obviously, things had gone wrong. The whole swindle depended upon Lewin Caspar remaining unsuspected. The moment the detectives learned that the robber was a friend of Lewin's father, "the game was up".

Two more accomplices were arrested: a go-between called

Emanuel Moses, and his daughter Alice Abrahams, who had
sold the gold-dust to Solomons. At the trial, it emerged that
there was little honour among thieves: everybody was apparently out to swindle everybody else. Henry Moss had made a
determined attempt to keep all the gold for himself, but was
forced to hand it over to Moses and his daughter. They sold it to
Solomons, who agreed to pay £3,700, but gave an IOU for
£1,800 of this, which he then refused to pay. Alice Abrahams
cheated her own father of £13 which she got for the gold dust
shaken out of the bottom of the empty bags; her father cheated
the Caspars by claiming he only received £2,000 for the gold.
The Caspars intended to cheat Henry Moss by fobbing him off
with an absurdly small part of the proceeds. And Moss –
indignant when he learned that he was being cheated –
decided to go to the police and give evidence against his

Around mid-1911, Paris was full of anarchists who declared that
the corrupt social system could only be overthrown by violence.
Among these was Jules Joseph Bonnot, the son of a poor family
who had educated himself, and who at one time had been a
racing driver. In Paris anarchist clubs Bonnot recruited a group of
fifteen idealistic young men who agreed to follow him to the
death. They obtained guns by raiding a gun shop, and stole a
large, fast car from a garage. On 21 December 1911, Bonnot and
four followers waylaid a bank messenger with typical brutality
and violence, shooting him first in the chest, then in the throat,
and firing shots over the heads of the crowd as they drove off.
Their haul proved to be small, consisting mostly of useless
securities. (Incredibly, the bank messenger recovered.)

When they knocked down a woman as they were driving a
stolen car, they drove off at top speed; a policeman who tried to
intercept them was shot to death.

In March 1912 they committed another typically brutal crime.
They needed a car, so they waylaid the Marquis de Rouge, who
was driving out of Paris in a new sports car at six in the morning.
Rouge and the chauffeur were both shot dead and dumped in a
ditch; the gangsters then drove to a bank in Chantilly, and while
Bonnot waited with the engine running, the others went into the
bank and fired indiscriminately, killing one man and seriously
wounding two more. As they rushed out with their haul, Bonnot was
trying to hold an angry crowd at bay by firing over their heads.

accomplices. (By this time, Moss had admitted that he knew he was involved in a crime from the beginning.) What seems certain is that if the Caspars had not tried to cheat Moss, he would never have gone to the police, and they would have gone free for lack of evidence.

Ellis Caspar and Emanuel Moses received fourteen years each, Lewin Caspar was transported for seven years, and Alice Abrahams received only four months, on the grounds that she had been influenced by her father. Henry Moss was sentenced to a day in prison.

This complicated affair – with its tale of mutual plunder – set all London laughing. No one noticed that something highly significant had happened: that a clerk in a position of trust had planned to become a wealthy man overnight with a brilliant and cunning scheme. If it had not been for the determination of

---

While they were driving away, a bullet grazed the arm of Francois Callemin; in a rage, he began shooting at random, luckily hitting no one. This robbery brought the gang its largest haul so far.

The Bonnot gang was now being hunted by the whole French police force, and the public clamoured for their arrest. More robberies followed, and the gang lived up to its reputation for brutal and unnecessary killings. One of them, Pierre Garnier – who had shot the bank messenger – wrote the police a defiant letter enclosing his fingerprints, and declaring: "I know you will get me eventually because you have force on your side, but I shall make you pay dearly for my life."

Other anarchists were shocked by all this violence, and the police began to receive tip-offs. Inspector Jouin arrested one gang member in March 1913, and another soon after. But Jouin himself was killed when he surprised Bonnot in a hideout in Ivry; Bonnot shot his way out, wounding another policeman.

Finally, Bonnot's hiding place at Choisy-le-Roi was surrounded after a tip-off from another hostile anarchist who felt that Bonnot was giving the cause a bad name. Dubois, the man who was sheltering Bonnot, was shot dead as he fired at the police while trying to escape on a motor bike. After six hours of shooting, the police stormed the house, and found Bonnot bleeding to death; he had time to shout "Bastards" as he lapsed into a coma.

Other gang members were arrested one by one, and many – including Callemin and Garnier – ended on the guillotine.

everyone involved to swindle everyone else, he might have succeeded. The gold-dust case is the first of the robberies that are usually preceded by the epithet "great".

The Great Bullion Robbery

It has to be admitted that the great gold-dust robbery lacks the stuff of high drama. This is certainly not true of the great gold bullion robbery that took place sixteen years later.

In fact, the story begins in 1848, when a remarkable theft occurred on the British railway; when a strong-box arrived by train in Bristol, the box was found forced open, and £1,500 in gold was missing. The case was never solved. But it attracted the attention – and admiration – of a suave gentleman forger named Edgar Agar. He knew that large quantities of gold bullion were sent by train, and that, with careful planning, he might make enough money to last him the rest of his life.

Agar was introduced to an unimpressive little clerk named William Pierce, who had sandy hair and a shifty look; Pierce worked for the South-Eastern Railway as a ticket printer, and he was a man of expensive tastes who never had the money to pay for them. So when Agar disclosed his interest in the gold shipments, Pierce showed himself eager to cooperate. He set out to learn all he could about the way the gold was sent, and at what point it might be vulnerable.

What Pierce learned was not encouraging. Large quantities of gold were often sent from London to Paris. But there were *two* keys to the heavy safe, and one was kept in London and the other in Folkestone. That obviously presented enormous difficulties to the most enterprising thief. Agar decided that forgery was easier, and dropped the idea.

In 1850, the shifty little clerk was discharged on suspicion of theft, which was probably justified. Now he was more anxious than ever to take part in the scheme. Accordingly he made the acquaintance of the station master at Margate, William George Tester, and persuaded him to help. This was in 1854, six years after Agar had dreamed up the plan. With Tester's help, it should be possible, he thought, to get a duplicate of both keys.

Map showing the details of a later Bullion robbery, May 1967

Agar, just back from America, where his criminal enterprises had flourished, thought this sounded promising. He and Pierce went off to Folkestone and took rooms there, then spent a great deal of time hanging around the station, trying to learn where the second key was kept. But the railway police noticed them, and took them for pickpockets. The down-at-heel Pierce fled back to London.

Agar stayed behind a short time longer, as he had scraped an acquaintance with the clerk in charge of the keys, a man called Sharman. The problem was how to find out which of the keys fitted the bullion safe. But the railway police were watchful, and warned Sharman that they thought Agar a villain. So Sharman suddenly ceased to respond to Agar's friendly overtures.

Agar now devised a clever scheme to find out about the key. He had £200 in gold sent from London to Folkestone, to be delivered to a Mr Archer – himself. This, of course, would be sent in the gold bullion safe. Then Agar went to Folkestone to collect it. The scheme should have failed, because Sharman had been warned about Agar. But luck was on Agar's side; Sharman was away on the day he called, and the young booking clerk went to the key cupboard – watched by Agar – and removed the gold bullion key. Obstacle number one had been successfully surmounted.

So was obstacle number two. Tester, the Margate station master, was transferred to London, and soon had the opportunity to take a wax impression of the other key. Now Pierce and Agar hurried back to Folkestone, and waited for the boat train to come in. For a few minutes, the office was empty while the various clerks came out and attended to the registered luggage. Pierce slipped into the office and grabbed the key; outside, Agar pressed it into a piece of soft wax. Within a minute, the key was back on its hook, and Agar and Pierce were strolling out of the station.

A fourth – and most essential – accomplice had now been enrolled – a guard named James Burgess, who was in charge of the guard's van that contained the bullion safes. Without him, the robbery would have been impossible. Burgess agreed that he would give a signal – wiping his hankerchief across his face – when there was gold bullion on the train.

Things were still far from straightforward. Both keys were cut from the wax impressions, but it took months – it was a complicated design – and when Agar tried them out, neither would fit. They had to modify them eight times before they would open the safe. Now that success was at last in sight, Pierce and Agar moved to new lodgings, and Pierce wore a false moustache and wig and changed his name.

There was still one more problem. Unless the stolen gold was replaced by something of equal weight, the loss might be discovered at Folkestone, where the bullion was weighed before it left England. That would be too soon. So Agar and Pierce bought two hundredweights of lead grapeshot from the Shot Tower, near Waterloo, packed it into carpet bags, and staggered back with these to their lodgings.

It was now the beginning of May 1855. Every evening the men followed the same routine. They drove to London Bridge Station in a cab, with their carpet bags, each weighing half a hundredweight, and then took up their position where they could watch the bullion train. But for two weeks, Burgess failed to make the signal they were waiting for, and they drove back home. They began to worry in case railway police should notice them again. But finally, on 15 May 1855, Burgess wiped his face with his handkerchief. Agar and Pierce immediately bought tickets, and went to the luggage van, where Burgess stowed their abnormally heavy bags. But only Pierce came out of the van. He went to a first class compartment. Agar crouched in a corner of the luggage van, covered with an apron.

As soon as the train started, Agar threw off the apron. From a leather bag strapped under his arm – and concealed by his cape-overcoat – he removed his tools: wedges, pincers, sealing wax and tapers. While Burgess acted as lookout, Agar opened the first of the two safes with the keys and removed two small and very heavy wooden boxes, sealed with metal bands. Working with feverish haste – the train would soon be stopping at Reigate – he used the wedges to prise up the bands on one of the boxes, then forced it open. It contained solid gold ingots. Four of these were removed, and bags of lead shot placed in the box. Then the nails were hammered down again and the bands replaced; finally, Agar lit a taper and melted the sealing wax to replace the seals. The box was locked back in the safe, and when the train stopped at Reigate, Burgess was ready to hand over a carpet bag to a man who came to the guard's van to claim it. William Tester strolled off the station carrying the four bars of gold.

As the train left Reigate, Pierce joined Agar in the guard's van, and they forced open the second box. This proved to contain American gold coins. Again, a quantity of these were removed and replaced with lead shot. After this, the second safe was opened. This was found to contain smaller gold bars. Regretfully – because he was running out of lead shot – Agar was forced to remove only a few of these. Their total haul was worth £12,000.

In Folkestone, two passengers holding carpet bags walked out of the station, climbed into another train, and continued their journey to Dover, where they arrived before midnight. There they went into a hotel and had a meal – their train back to London left at two in the morning. While Pierce guarded the bags, Agar took a stroll along the dock and dropped the safe keys and the tools into the water.

At the station, a porter offered to take their bags; when they declined, he became suspicious, and asked to see their tickets. But Agar had thought of everything, and produced two Ostend

William L. Carlisle – known as the "White Bandit" – stands out as one of the most amiable robbers in American history. Between 1916 and 1919, he robbed numerous passenger train across the east and central United States. Donning a handkerchief to hide his face and waving a revolver, he would relieve passengers of their valuables in much the same way as any other petty crook, but with one important difference: he would not steal from women. At times panicked ladies would even thrust their purses and jewellery at him, but he would always courteously refuse.

On one occasion, seeing that a man had only raised a single hand when commanded he moved closer to threaten him. However, he then saw that the victim had only one arm. Carlisle immediately apologised and left the man with his belongings.

His flamboyance was amazing. He not only wrote to the police to ask how the investigation was going, he even told them which trains he was going to rob beforehand. Even with this help, it took the authorities some time to catch him, and then he promptly escaped.

He was eventually recaptured and served seventeen years before being paroled in 1936. On release he turned over a new leaf, got a job and married. For the rest of his life he devoted all his spare time to campaigning against crime. Speaking at many public rallies he stressed the need to help young offenders, not to castigate them.

tickets – the return halves. The porter thanked him – then remembered that there had been no Ostend boat that day, and asked them when they came from Ostend. ("Yesterday") said Agar breezily, holding out a tip. The porter saluted and went away.

Two hours later they were back in London. Even now they continued to take precautions. In case they had been followed, they took three cabs in succession, arriving back at their lodgings after dawn. There Tester was waiting with his carpet bag. After seven years of planning, the great bullion robbery was now successfully completed.

Meanwhile, in the Gare Maritime in Boulogne, the cross-Channel steamer lay alongside the quay, and in the Customs shed officials were checking the weight of the three iron-bound boxes against the documents that accompanied them. In fact, the boxes had been weighed at Folkestone, and one had been found to be light; but since the other was too heavy, the Folkestone Customs had decided that a simple mistake had been made. The Boulogne authorities were less casual. When it was realised that two out of three boxes were under-weight, there was deep suspicion. Customs officials re-checked the papers; there could be no possible doubt; the boxes were dozens of pounds lighter than they should be. When the boxes were finally opened, and the lead shot discovered, there was consternation. The seals were intact. But on closer examination, the officials discovered the marks of the wedges and pincers that revealed that the boxes had been opened . . .

Back in London, the gang converted around £400 in American gold sovereigns into English money, and it was divided equally.

The gold was now moved from the temporary lodgings to Agar's house in Shepherds Bush. Here he lived with a young woman called Fanny Kay, whom he had met working behind the counter in the buffet at Tonbridge station, and persuaded to move in with him. She had borne him a son. For the next week or so, Agar and Pierce worked at a furnace in the upper room, converting the gold ingots into smaller ones by running the gold into iron moulds. They sliced up some of the smaller ingots with a hammer and chisel. These smaller pieces they were able to sell at £3 an ounce, bringing in £300. Then, very slowly and cautiously, Agar began looking around for a customer for a larger part of the loot. Tester and Burgess were both given a share of the proceeds, after Agar had impressed upon them the importance of continuing in their jobs and displaying no sign of sudden affluence. A famous forger named James Townesend Saward – better known as Jim the Penman – bought £2,500-worth of the gold.

At this moment, Agar's luck turned – although he was not aware of it at the time. In spite of his new wealth, he continued in his old occupation of forging. He came across a young man named Smith, who seemed bright and willing, and employed him to do odd jobs. Smith seemed to be reliable – several lots of money were safely delivered by him – so Agar decided to employ the young man on a permanent basis. Although Smith was not told this, his job was to go to banks and cash forged cheques. In case Smith was caught, Agar made sure that he personally was untraceable; Smith did not know his real name, and he always met him at a hotel.

What Agar did not know was that Smith had spent twelve months in jail for receiving stolen goods, and had run a brothel, which had gone bankrupt. When Smith told a thief called William Humphries about his new job, Humphries advised him to be very careful, since Agar was a villain. In fact, Humphries himself had reason to dislike Agar. The latter had a roving eye, and had seduced Humphries's mistress, a girl named Emily Campbell. Fanny had found out, and after a quarrel, Agar had walked out on her and taken his new mistress to live with him elsewhere.

When Smith realised that he had been selected so that he could take all the risk, he went to the police. And the police arranged a trap. One day, Agar sent Smith to a bank in Lombard Street with a forged cheque for £700. Agar followed – in the event of Smith being caught, he wanted to make sure he was ready to disappear. The bank, apparently, handed over the £700 without suspicion; in fact, they had been tipped off by the police, and filled the bag with farthings. Smith then met his employer – whom he knew as Captain Pellatt – in Jockey's Fields (now Grays Inn) and handed over the bag. At this moment the police pounced and arrested them both. Agar was charged with forging the £700 cheque.

Agar was convinced that Humphries had "framed" him for stealing his mistress, and protested his innocence. But counterfeit notes and forged plates in his home made it clear that he was a professional crook. He was sentenced to transportation for life in Botany Bay. This was only five months after the great bullion robbery.

Now he began to feel remorse about abandoning Fanny Kay

and their son. He had £15,000 in the bank, and decided to settle it on Fanny. But he wanted to invest it and give Fanny a weekly income, rather than handing her the whole sum – being unaccustomed to handling money, she would probably spend it, whereas it could bring her an income of £2 a week for life. Agar now made his greatest mistake so far: he decided to entrust Pierce with the business of investing the money and making sure that Fanny received her income: the deed was signed in the Portland Convict Prison, where Agar was awaiting transportation. But the slippery Pierce had no intention of investing the money; since Fanny had not been told about it, he felt there was nothing to stop him from keeping it for himself.

In due course, Agar wrote to Fanny, asking her to buy a silver cup for his son, and another for Pierce's child; he also asked for a geography book with a section on Australia. Pierce, he said, would give her the money. Fanny – who was living with Pierce and his wife – asked him for money, but Pierce refused. Fanny stormed out, and went to the governor of Newgate prison, where Agar had originally been held. She had suspected what had been going on in the upper room with the furnace (although she knew nothing of the robbery), and wanted to make sure that Pierce went to jail too.

When a solicitor from the South-Eastern Railway arrived at Portland prison, and told Agar what was happening to his mistress and child, Agar was at first incredulous, then furious. Encouraged by the solicitor, he went on to tell the full story of the great bullion robbery. Pierce was arrested, and thousands of pounds were found buried under his front step and hidden in his pantry.

On 12 January 1857, Pierce, Tester and Burgess stood in front of the judge at the Bailey, and were duly sentenced – Burgess and Tester to fourteen years transportation to Botany Bay, and Pierce – amazingly enough – to a mere two years; Pierce had been charged as a member of the railway company, which he was not, and a lawyer was able to obtain a shorter sentence on this technicality. The judge said some extremely harsh words at his sentencing, but could do nothing about it. At least the judge succeeded in restoring Agar's money to Fanny Kay, who thereupon became rich.

Agar served five years of his sentence and was released, whereupon he married Fanny Kay. Unfortunately, he returned to crime, and was transported once more to Botany Bay. Shortly before his death, a convict who had recently arrived told him that he had become a legend in the London underworld; Agar groaned: "That means nothing at all."

Fanny herself died penniless in a workhouse. What happened to Pierce is not known, except that he was badly beaten up after he was released from jail – no doubt at Agar's request.

Tester, at least, succeeded in making good; after being released from prison in Australia, he started a highly successful grocery business, and ended a wealthy man.

The Case of Orrock's Chisel

Unlike the previous two cases, the case that follows is of a burglary that went appallingly wrong. But it has become one of the great classics of Victorian detection.

On 1 December 1882, the cobbled, gaslit streets of east London were wrapped in choking fog as a young constable set out from Dalston police station on a beat that took him down a narrow thoroughfare called Ashwin Street. As he turned the corner, he came to a sudden halt as he saw a man placing a lantern on top of the wall outside the Baptist chapel, and beginning to scramble over. PC Cole took a swift step forward, laid his hand on the man's shoulder, and asked: "What do you think you're doing?" For a moment, the man – who seemed little more than a youth – looked as if he was going to resist; then he changed his mind and agreed to "go quietly". But PC Cole and his captive had only gone as far as the pub on the corner when the man broke loose and ran. Cole ran after him and grabbed him by the left arm; as he did so, the man reached into his pocket, pulled out a revolver, and fired three shots. A woman who was walking towards them screamed and fled; as she ran, she heard another shot. Moments later, she encountered two policeman in Dalston Lane, and led them back to the scene of the shooting. PC Cole was lying on the pavement outside the Baptist chapel, his head in the gutter; a trickle of blood ran from the bullet hole behind his left ear. He died five minutes after being admitted to the local German Hospital.

Inspector Glass, who took charge of the case, ordered a search of the area where the policeman had been found; on the wall of the Baptist chapel, the burglar had left his dark lantern; behind the railings, a chisel, a jemmy, and a wooden wedge had ben left on the ground. The only other clue was a black billycock hat, which the burglar had lost in the course of the struggle. The woman who had seen him running away described him as short and slightly built; another witness gave the same description.

There was one man in the Dalston police station who believed he knew the identity of the murderer. Only minutes before Cole had arrested the burglar, Police Sergeant Cobb had been walking along Ashwin Street with another sergeant, Branwell, when they had noticed a man standing under a streetlamp. Cobb recognized him as a young cabinetmaker named Tom Orrock, and when he saw the policeman, he looked furtive and uncomfortable. Orrock had no criminal record, but he kept bad company – thugs and professional criminals – and it seemed a reasonable assumption that he would one day try his hand at crime. As they passed Orrock that night, Cobb had been tempted to arrest him for loitering. But standing under a streetlamp was no crime, and Cobb had decided against it. Now he regretted it, and was inclined to blame himself for the death of PC Cole, who was a young married man with children.

Informed of Sergeant Cobb's suspicions, Inspector Glass was inclined to be dismissive – to begin with, he disliked Cobb, regarding him as too unimaginative and too conscientious. But he ordered Tom Orrock – who was nineteen – to be brought in for an identity parade. When the witnesses who had glimpsed Cole's captive failed to identify him, Orrock was released. Soon after that, he disappeared from his usual haunts.

Months after the murder, the investigation was at a standstill. The clues seemed to lead nowhere. The hat bore no marks of identification, and the chisels and the large wooden wedge might have belonged to anybody. But the bullets looked more promising. All four had been recovered – two from the policeman's skull, one from his truncheon, another from the truncheon case. They were unusual in that they had been fired from a revolver that was little more than a toy – the kind of thing ladies sometimes carried in their handbags. The science of ballistics was unknown in 1882, but the rarity of the gun suggested that it might one day provide a valuable piece of evidence.

When studied through a magnifying glass, one of the chisels also yielded an interesting clue. A series of scratches near the handle looked like an attempt at writing, probably with a sharp nail. And when the chisel was photographed for the case file, the letters could be seen more clearly, and they resolved themselves into a capital R, followed by what looked like an o, a c, and a k. Rock. Could it be short for Orrock? Cobb began calling in every tool shop in the Hackney and Dalston area, asking if they recognized the chisels, but met with no success.

Cobb refused to give up. A year after the murder, he was talking with an acquaintance of the missing cabinetmaker named Henry Mortimer, who occasionally acted as a police informer. And Mortimer's rambling discourse suddenly arrested the sergeant's attention when he mentioned that Tom Orrock had possessed a revolver – a nickel-plated, pin-fire miniature affair, Orrock had seen it advertised in the *Exchange and Mart*, and he and Mortimer had gone to Tottenham to purchase it from the owner for the sum of half a guinea. They had also been accompanied by two men named Miles and Evans, both professional – if unsuccessful – criminals. On the way home, the four men had stopped on Tottenham Marshes and used a tree for target practice. At Cobb's request, Mortimer accompanied him to Tottenham and showed him the tree. The following day, Cobb returned alone, and dug some bullets out of the tree with his penknife. One of them was relatively undamaged, and was obviously of the same calibre as the bullets that had been fired at PC Cole.

Now Cobb was sure he had his man, and that view was confirmed when Mortimer admitted that Orrock had virtually confessed to killing PC Cole. When Mortimer had expressed disbelief, Orrock had replied: "If they can prove it against me, I'm willing to take the consequences." This is precisely what Cobb now set out to do.

The first step was to lay the new evidence before his immediate superior. Inspector Glass was still inclined to be indifferent, but he agreed to ask for help from New Scotland Yard in trying to trace the shop that had sold the chisel. And, it was the Scotland Yard team that finally located a woman named Preston, a widow who carried on her husband's tool-sharpening business. She recognized the chisel because she always made a practice of scratching the name of the owner near the handle; she remembered the young man who brought in the chisel for grinding had given the name Orrock, which she had shortened to "Rock".

Now at last, they had the kind of evidence that might impress a jury. All that remained was to locate Tom Orrock. Scotland Yard was asked to circulate his description to every police station in the country. This would normally have brought prompt results, for in those days before the population explosion, most police stations were aware of any strangers who had moved into their district. So when another year failed to bring news of the wanted man, Glass was inclined to assume either that he was dead or that he had gone abroad. Cobb refused to believe it. And one day he had an inspiration. One place where a man could "lie low" with reasonable chance of escaping recognition was prison. Once again, Cobb began painstaking enquiries – enquiries that entitle him to be ranked with Canler and Macé as a distinguished practitioner of the needle-in-the-haystack method. And he soon learned that a man answering Orrock's description had been serving a term for burglary in Coldbath Fields for the past two years. Coldbath Fields, in Farringdon Road, was one of London's newer prisons, and had a reputation for severity. The name under which the prisoner was serving his sentence was not Tom Orrock, and when he was summoned to the governor's office, the man denied that he was called Orrock or had ever been in Dalston. Sergeant Cobb attended an identity parade, and had to admit reluctantly that he was unable to recognize Orrock among the seven uniformed convicts who now faced him. But as the men filed out again, they passed under a light, and Cobb suddenly recognized the profile of the man he had last seen standing under a gaslamp in Dalston more that two years earlier. He stepped forward and laid his hand on the shoulder of Thomas Henry Orrock.

Now it was a question of building up the web of circumstantial evidence. Orrock's sister, Mrs Bere, was questioned, and admitted that on the night of the murder her brother had returned home with a torn trouser leg, and without his hat, claiming that he had been involved in a street brawl. Orrock's two friends Miles and Evans were questioned separately. They admitted that they had spent the day of the murder drinking with Tom Orrock in various pubs, and that soon after 10 o'clock in the evening, the three had been in the Railway Tavern in Ashwin Street when Orrock boasted that he intended to embark on a criminal career by "cracking a crib" – stealing the silver plate of the Baptist church, which he attended regularly, and taking it to his brother-in-law to be melted down. Orrock had then left the pub. Not long after, Miles and Evans heard the sound of revolver shots, but claimed they had taken them for fog signals. All the same, they had left the pub and been among the crowd that gathered around the wounded policeman. Three weeks later, when a reward of £200 had been offered for information leading to the capture of the murderer, Orrock went to Evans and begged him not to inform on him; Evans swore that he would not "ruck" on a comrade even for a thousand pounds.

But all this was merely hearsay evidence. The vital link between Tom Orrock and the murder of PC Cole was the revolver. This had disappeared – one witness said that Orrock admitted throwing it into the River Lea. But the police were able to track down the man who had sold Orrock the revolver – his name was McLellan – and he unhesitatingly identified bullets and cartridge cases as being the calibre of those he had sold to a young man in the last week of November 1882, one week before the murder. McLellan's description of the purchaser fitted Thomas Henry Orrock.

A few decades later, all this corroborative evidence would have been unnecessary. Examination of the bullets under a comparison microscope would have proved that the bullet found in the tree at Tottenham was identical with the bullet that killed PC Cole.

But in the year 1884, no one had yet thought of studying the pattern of rifle marks on the side of a bullet; it would be another five years before Edmond Locard's mentor, Professor Alexandre Lacassagne, would provide the evidence to convict a murderer by studying bullet grooves under a microscope. Nevertheless, when Tom Orrock came to trial in September 1884, it was the bullet evidence that carried most weight with the jury. The bullet found in the tree at Tottenham was "precisely similar to the one found in the brain of the dead constable", said the prosecution. "If the prisoner purchased the revolver, where was it? A man did not throw away a revolver that cost him 10 shillings without good cause." The jury was convinced. On Saturday 20 September 1884, Thomas Orrock was convicted of the murder of PC Cole and sentenced to be hanged. The jury added a special recommendation to Sergeant Cobb for his persistence in tracking down the killer. But the chronicler relates that, in after years, Inspector Glass liked to claim credit for capturing Orrock, and "has often remarked that the man who in reality put the police in possession of their information to this day is ignorant that he disclosed to them this knowledge" – from which it would appear that Glass continued to resent the success of his subordinate and to deny him any of the credit.

chapter four

THE AGE OF DETECTION

Fingerprints

The greatest single advance in crime-fighting was the discovery of fingerprints. As long ago as the 1820s, it had been noticed that no two fingerprints are ever alike. But what good was that when there was no method of classifying them? This had to wait until the 1890s, when Sir Francis Galton and Edward Henry finally worked out a way of classifying them according to "loops" "arches" and "whorls". But it was not until 1902 that Henry set up a fingerprint system at Scotland Yard. It proved its value on Derby Day, 1902, when the police were able to prove that twenty-nine arrested men were pickpockets with previous convictions. Later the same year, a burglar named Henry Jackson was caught when he left his fingerprints on some fresh paint in a house in Denmark Hill.

The first major crime solved by fingerprints in England was committed by two brothers named Alfred and Edward Stratton; early in the morning of 27 March 1905, they broke into a shop in Deptford, East London, hoping to find a large sum of money. They knocked out the shopkeeper and his wife with a jemmy, hitting them so violently that both died. But Alfred Stratton left behind a fingerprint on the cash box – in which there had only been a few pounds – and both brothers were hanged.

The Great Bertillon

In France, fingerprinting took longer to establish itself; this was largely because the French had already invented their own method of criminal identification, called "Bertillonage", after its inventor, Alphonse Bertillon.

Bertillon's story would be ideal for Hollywood. He compared photographs of criminals to see if there was some way of classifying noses and faces. Then he thought it might be a good idea to take measurements of criminals when they were arrested – height, reach, circumference of head, height sitting down, length of left hand, left foot, left leg – Bertillon chose the left-hand side because it was unlikely to be affected by work. He was subject to constipation, stomach upsets, headaches and nosebleeds; but he had a certain stubbornness that made him ignore the knowing smiles of colleagues. A doctor named Adolphe Quetelet had asserted that the chances of two people being exactly the same height are four to one. If that was so, and the same thing applied to the other statistics, then you needed only two or three measurements of each criminal to raise the odds to a hundred to one. When the prefect of police ignored Bertillon's letter about this method, Bertillon bought himself a set of filing cards, and started to work on his own, staying in the office until late at night. Macé revealed a lack of insight when he read Bertillon's report, and said it was too theoretical. The prefect, Andrieux, told Bertillon to stop making a nuisance of himself. And three years went by before Bertillon could persuade a new prefect Jean Camecasse to give him an interview. Camecasse was as sceptical as his predecessor, but he was impressed by the clerk's persistence. He told Bertillon that they would introduce his method experimentally for three months. This was obviously absurd; it would take more than three months to build up a file, and a method like Bertillon's depended on accumulation. He knew his only chance lay in working on and praying for luck. His card index swelled at the rate of a few hundred a month. But with more than twenty thousand criminals in Paris alone, the chances of identifying one of them was low. Towards the end of the third month, Bertillon had towards two thousand cards. Theoretically, his chance of identification was one in ten – fairly high. But it must be remembered that a large number of his criminals were sent to jail, often for years, so most of his file was lying fallow, so to speak.

On 20 February 1883, luck was with him. His system led him to identify a petty criminal who had been measured three months earlier. It was a very small triumph, but it was enough to make Camecasse decide to allow the experiment to continue. This was not far-sightedness. The post of prefect was a political appointment; Camecasse was hoping for fame. Unfortunately, a new prefect had been appointed by the time Bertillon became a celebrity; but history allows Camecasse the credit. As the file swelled, identification became more frequent. Before long, it averaged one a day.

Bertillon's system was soon being used by most of the major police forces of the world. And when fingerprinting arrived, Bertillon immediately incorporated this into his system, making sure that the file on every criminal included his fingerprints. Unfortunately, Bertillon refused to face up to the truth: that fingerprinting had completely superseded his own methods.

On 22 July 1934, John Dillinger, a farm boy turned bank robber, went to the Biograph cinema in Chicago with his girlfriend Polly Hamilton and her friend Anna Sage to see Clark Gable in *Manhattan Melodrama*. Anna Sage, who was under threat of deportation, had decided to try and curry favour with the authorities by betraying the gangster, and was wearing a bright red dress. As they left the cinema, FBI agents surrounded him, and as Dillinger sprinted away, three agents fired, killing him.

But did he really die? The autopsy notes reveal that the corpse's eyes were brown; Dillinger's were blue. The dead man suffered from a heart condition; Dillinger did not. Neither did the corpse possess various marks and scars that Dillinger was known to have on his body.

Crime writer Jay Robert Nash has argued that the dead man was a small-time hoodlum called Jimmy Lawrence, and that J. Edgar Hoover was too embarrassed to acknowledge the mistake. Lawrence, he believes, was "set up" by the "lady in red" so Dillinger could escape. A fellow gang member, Blackie Audett, claims that Dillinger married and escaped to Oregon. The rest of Dillinger's gang was wiped out not long after their leader's "death".

He refused to take the obvious step and classify fingerprints so they could be identified immediately. If a French policeman wished to identify a burglar who had left his fingerprint at the scene of a crime, he had to go through every single file until he found it. It was the sheer cumbersomeness of this method that led to Bertillon's downfall.

The Theft of the Mona Lisa

On 21 August 1911, someone stole Leonardo's *Mona Lisa* from the Louvre. It should, of course, have been a total impossibility, with so many guards; but it happened on a Monday, when the Louvre was closed to the public. The painting, which is on a panel, was housed in a case with a glass cover. This case was found, empty, on the service stairs.

Bertillon was immediately summoned, and careful examination revealed fingerprints. A fingerprint is made by sweat – that is to say, the skin's secretions which include fatty substances; this comes from sweat pores along the papillary ridges, and also from contact of the fingertips with parts of the body where there are sebaceous glands, such as the face. Latent or invisible prints on smooth surfaces can be made visible by dusting the surface with fine powder, such as talc, aluminium, or lead powder. (On white surfaces, such as china, a black powder is used.) And when Bertillon dusted the glass with powder, he realized with delight that the thief had left behind a good set of fingerprints. And now if the thief happened to have a criminal record, it should be a matter of the utmost simplicity to identify him . . .

And if the theft had taken place in London or Berlin or Madrid, it would have been. But Bertillon's fingerprints were still unclassified. And since 1902, when he had solved the Scheffer case, he had accumulated more than 100,000 additional cards. So, in fact, it was an impossible task. Bertillon and his assistants searched for weeks and months – Bertillon was such an obsessive that he probably went through every card individually. But after a few hundred prints, the eyes grow tired, and the attention flags. Bertillon must have ended day

after day in a state of exhausted defeat. Nothing could have
brought home to him more clearly that his system was a waste
of time, and that he should have adopted Henry's fingerprint
classification, as improved by Inspector Collins.

Two years later, the thief was arrested in Florence. The police
had been tipped off by an art dealer named Alfredo Geri, who
had been offered the painting in a letter signed "Leonard".
Leonard proved to be an Italian house painter named Vicenzo
Perrugia, and he was carrying the *Mona Lisa* with him. His story
of the theft caused astonishment, and some amusement at the
expense of the Louvre authorities. The crime had not been
planned. Perrugia had been a friend of a painter working in the
Louvre, and the guards were familiar with him; they let him
past without question. Finding himself quite alone in the Salon
Carré with the famous painting, the temptation had been too
much. He had simply lifted the case off the wall, walked down
the service staircase, and extracted the painting, leaving his
fingerprints on the glass. Then he had hidden the painting –
which is small – beneath his smock and walked out unchal-
lenged. For the next two years the *Mona Lisa* lay hidden under
his bed.

John Dillinger 1934

But for Bertillon, the final bitterness must have been that he had Perrugia's card in his file, for Perrugia was a petty thief who had been arrested several times.

Significantly, in this same year 1913, Bertillon was found to be suffering from pernicious anaemia; he died in February 1914, and France immediately accepted the same fingerprint classification as the rest of the world.

The Great Pearl Robbery

In fact, fingerprint evidence played no part in the most famous robbery of 1913, which was a kind of throw-back to the "great" robberies of the Victorian age.

The story begins on 16 July 1913, in the office of a diamond merchant called Max Mayer, in Hatton Garden. Mr Mayer was anxious to go away on holiday, but first he wanted to replace in his safe his most precious possession: a pearl necklace worth £130,000, which he had built up over many years. The necklace had been in Paris, in the hands of a dealer named Henri Salomons, who had been showing it to a wealthy customer. Unfortunately, the deal had fallen through, and the necklace had been returned back to Mr Mayer by registered post. This was not the first time that the famous necklace – whose existence was known to the whole of the jewellery trade – had been back and forth across the Channel, and so far, it had been perfectly safe.

But when Mr Mayer opened the sealed package on that July morning just before the First World War, he was shocked to find that it contained only several lumps of sugar. Scotland Yard was notified immediately, and a telegram despatched to M. Salomons in Paris. He immediately rushed to London, and confirmed that he and his wife had packed the pearls themselves, and sent them from the local post office in the Rue de Provence. Salomons was above suspicion. So it was obvious that the necklace had been stolen in transit. The sugar lumps were French, which suggested that the substitution had taken place in France, probably on the mail train. Clearly, the theft had been carefully planned, for the package had been re-sealed with identical string, and with sealing-wax that bore Mr Mayer's seal, MM.

The Paris police were also informed, and immediately began tracing the passage of the necklace from the post office to the Cross-Channel ferry. They ended by admitting their bafflement. There was simply no point at which the registered package could have been opened.

Fortunately for Mr Mayer, the necklace was insured. Nevertheless, it was his most precious possession, and he longed – against all the odds – for its return. Mr Mayer therefore offered a £10,000 reward for its recovery.

To the delight of Scotland Yard, this worked. They received a letter from an Antwerp jewel dealer named Samuel Brandstater, who said he and his cousin Meyer Quadratstein – another diamond merchant – had been offered the necklace. In due course, Brandstater and Quatratstein arrived at Scotland Yard. Brandstater then explained that he had been contacted by a relative from London, a diamond broker named Leiser Gutwirth, who had offered him the pearl necklace – admitting it was stolen – for one and a half million francs. Brandstater had offered 300,000 francs, which Gutwirth had indignantly rejected. So Brandstater told him he would try and raise more money, and Gutwirth had returned to London.

So now Scotland Yard knew the name of at least one of the thieves. And now that Brandstater had betrayed his relative, they could rely on his help to recover the necklace and earn the reward. But the whole transaction obviously required care. If the thieves suspected they were betrayed, they would scatter, and Mr Mayer would never see the return of his necklace.

Now began the long and nerve-wracking business that Chief Inspector Ward of Scotland Yard – who was in charge of the case – called "playing the fish". First the informer Brandstater met Gutwirth at Charing Cross station, and raised his offer to half a millon francs. Gutwirth replied angrily: "Go back to Paris. The necklace cannot be bought at less than a million francs." Brandstater said he would try and raise more money, and agreed to meet Gutwirth again.

And so it went on – meetings at Gutwirth's home, at Lyons tea-shops, and various hotels. Usually, two policemen were sitting a few tables away, carefully observing everything. One by one, the other members of the gang revealed themselves. They were all "diamond merchants" who were also known to the police as high-powered crooks: Simon Silverman, Joseph

Grizzard and James Lockett. The police (and insurance company) enlisted the aid of a Paris diamond merchant named Max Spanier, who agreed to meet the thieves and make them an offer. At one meeting in a Strand tea-shop, Grizzard asked Lockett: "Have you got a match?", and Lockett tossed him a match box. Grizzard opened this and revealed three beautiful pearls lying in cotton wool. This was merely to prove that they really had the pearl necklace.

To convince the crooks that he was serious, Spanier bought two of the pearls for 50,000 francs each, and promised to buy the rest in a few days' time. Spanier, Brandstater and his cousin Quadratstein knew they were taking their lives in their hands every time they met the crooks in some hotel room, and the police provided them with loaded revolvers.

Unfortunately, the members of the Scotland Yard team were not all equally skilful at the art of shadowing. One day, the crooks spotted four obvious plain-clothes policemen watching the hotel. They lost no time in fleeing to the Continent, and for a while it looked as if the clumsiness of the police had destroyed months of patient work. But after a few weeks, the crooks were lulled once more into a sense of security, and when Spanier told

Captured booze during the Prohibition – 1921

them that he had a wealthy Indian prince who was interested in the necklace, they allowed themselves to be lured back to London. This time, Scotland Yard pounced immediately. It was at the British Museum tube station, and Gutwirth, Silverman, Lockett and Grizzard were all present when the police quietly took their arms and told them they were under arrest.

But now once again there was dismay at Scotland Yard. The thieves were not carrying the pearls. And although the police had enough evidence to convict them – the two pearls sold to Spanier – the case would certainly be counted a failure if the rest of the necklace was not recovered.

Then, totally unexpectedly, the necklace turned up – lying in the gutter in St Paul's Road, Highbury. A piano-maker named Horne picked up a match box wrapped in paper, and found that it contained some white beads. He took them to the local police station, where the police agreed they were probably valueless. When he got home, Horne found that one of the beads had fallen into his pocket, and in the local pub, offered it to anyone who wanted to buy it for the price of a pint – one penny. No one did. And later, Horne lost it. In fact the missing pearl was the largest in the necklace, and was worth thousands of pounds. It was never recovered.

The Highbury police finally realized that the box of ''beads'' might be the missing pearls that everyone was talking about, and asked someone from Scotland Yard to come and look at them. And so Mr Mayer finally received back most of his necklace, minus its largest pearl.

Now the story slowly emerged. The gang, led by Silverman, often ate in a Hatton Garden restaurant known as the ''Diamond Club'', where diamond brokers met and talked shop. It was there that they planned the coup – almost certainly overhearing Mr Mayer telling someone that his necklace was on its way back from Paris. But how could they get their hands on it? The answer was simple and obvious. When the necklace was on its way back, in a registered parcel bearing French stamps, the postman merely had to be bribed to take it to Silverman's office, where it would be opened and re-sealed. A craftsman had even made a replica of Mayer's MM seal for a shilling. Sugar would be substituted for the pearls – French sugar, to give the impression that the substitution had taken place in France – and the postman would then deliver it to Mr Mayer's office, and collect his receipt.

The gang refused to admit that there had been a postman

involved, but Gutwirth had told the informer Brandstater that £400 had been set aside as "expenses", to pay two postmen £200 each. No postman was ever charged as an accomplice.

The gang was let off surprisingly lightly. Lockett and Grizzard received seven years each, Silverman (who planned it) a mere five years, and Gutwirth only eighteen months, because he had no police record.

The final puzzle remains: how did the pearls end up in a London gutter? The answer, almost certainly, is that the gang had given them into the care of some accomplice, who heard that the thieves had been arrested, and suspected that he was next on the list. When the piano-maker Horne picked up the packet, he saw a man and a woman just climbing on to a nearby bus, and called to them to ask if they had dropped it; they did not reply. No one has ever learned whether the pearls were dropped in the gutter by accident or design, and Mr Mayer certainly did not care one way or the other.

The First Cat-Burglar

Fingerprinting had the effect of making burglars more careful. The old-fashioned Bill Sikes, with his checked cap and jemmy, was soon an endangered species, and a new and more sophisticated type of burglar appeared on the scene. The first to draw the attention of Scotland Yard is described by ex-Superintendent Robert Fabian, in his book *Fabian of the Yard*.

> Robert Augustus Delaney will be remembered at Scotland Yard as the man who started a new fashion in crime that was to become known as "cat-burglary". Delaney trod the crags and precipices of Park Lane's roofs with nonchalant skill. Wearing faultless evening clothes, he could apparently climb the sheer side of a house. I think he imagined himself a kind of acrobatic Raffles.
>
> He certainly made the great criminals of the past – like Charles Peace, who carried a collapsible ladder disguised as a bundle of firewood – look clumsy. In

his pocket was a slender steel tool like a putty-knife for slipping window catches – it could also open jewel-boxes. Around his trimly tailored waist coiled four yards of black silk rope. Two men died trying to imitate Delaney: "Irish Mac" impaled himself on spiked railings, and "The Doctor" – who should have known better – fell forty feet from a portico in St James's. He had £8,000 of jewels in his pocket and crawled grimly for two miles before dying.

In 1924, when the rich and noble residents of Park Lane were trooping splendidly in to dinner, Delaney would crouch beneath their windows, unwinding his gossamer rope. The tinkle of polished cutlery . . . or was it the clink of a dulled steel hook catching in the balcony drain gutter . . . and Gussie Delaney robbed their bedrooms like a wraith and departed before coffee wafted fragrantly into the victim's drawing-room and cigar smoke hazed the wine.

The thefts were reported to us in Vine Street, where I was a probationer detective fresh from training school. We questioned indignant flunkeys, far haughtier than their masters, but they knew nothing, and next week another robbery from a Park Lane bedroom – and so on at weekly intervals.

It was not really my case, nor was my probationer pal, Tommy Symes (now Chief Inspector), assigned to it. One night we sat stirring police-canteen coffee, waiting to go out on a routine club raid, but the Park Lane mystery burglaries intrigued us more.

"One each week for the past five weeks," I said. "A total of £30,000. He should be ready to retire soon. And none of us will have caught a whiff of him!"

Tommy leaned forward. "Keep it to yourself," he murmured. "I've been putting in some spare-time work on those burglaries – I've been making a sort of map . . ."

I had to laugh. "So have I, Tommy!" We compared efforts, and found that both of us had the same idea – a map of the Park Lane district, indicating those houses where residents were known to be outstandingly wealthy and where the dining-room could be kept under observation.

"And it looks as if he's working in some sort of sequence, too," I said quickly. "See – top end of Park Lane, then the bottom end, then St James's. Fourth burglary top of Park Lane again, fifth burglary at the bottom end . . ."

"And the next one around here!" Tommy's broad thumb covered Arlington Street at the Ritz Hotel corner. "It might be tonight," he added.

We left the canteen and went into the CID main room. The duty inspector called: "Oh, you two – that club job – it's off for tonight. We shan't be needing you."

We looked at each other. It was a crisp, starlit October evening, just gone dark. "Care for a bit of fresh air, Tommy?" I asked casually. He grinned. "Green Park it is!"

Concealed in the shadow and shrubbery of Green Park, we knew we could keep watch on the backs of all those tempting mansions by the Ritz corner. Three hours later we were chilled, cramped, disap-

---

For a brief period in the 1920s, the gang led by brothers Matt and George Kimes and Ray Terrill was one of the most successful in America. The members were all farm boys, many of whom had decided that bootlegging was more profitable than ploughing.

Terrill persuaded the Kimes brothers that bank robbery would be even more profitable than bootlegging, and so it proved. A raid at the Farmer's National Bank in Beggs, Oklahoma, netted $20,000. They were captured when their car hit a tree but Terrill and Matt Kimes escaped and robbed the same bank again, this time taking $18,000.

In Pampa, Texas, in 1927, the gang learned that the huge old iron bank safe was almost uncrackable, so they rolled it outside – while customers were held up by other gang members – loaded it on to a truck and drove away with it. It proved to contain $35,000.

Matt Kimes was caught soon after this and sentenced to life. Terrill teamed up with Herman Barker, eldest of Ma Barker's sons, but in September 1927, after a shoot-out during which they escaped, Barker was found dead in a ditch. (Ma Barker always claimed he had been "executed" by the police.) Terrill was captured soon after and spent most of his life behind bars.

pointed. Nothing had happened.

The next night was cloudy. Once again Tommy took the Green Park bandstand, while I waited in the garden behind Wimborne House. Faintly we heard the austere chimes of dinner gongs from the big mansions. One by one, bedroom lights winked out from costly chandeliers. I fumbled for a peppermint and stared into the shadows until my eyes felt aglow like a stoat's . . . A dark figure was creeping along the nearest garden boundary. Quick, agile as a cat, it vaulted the high railing and disappeared.

We next saw the shadowy intruder flit across one of the white balconies. How did he get up there? Tommy, flattened against the wall beneath the balcony, turned as I crept near him.

"Did you see that?" His voice was hoarse with suppressed excitement. "Like a blooming cat!"

"I'll wait for him here," I whispered. "You give the alarm inside."

The lights began to flash on in each of the spacious upstairs rooms as Tommy Symes raced through the bedrooms and corridors, with alarmed householders behind him. I heard excited voices – then the re-peated thud of sturdy shoulders at an equally sturdy thick mahogany door. The thief had jammed it with a wooden wedge, ready for such an emergency. He reappeared on the balcony, made no attempt to descend into the garden, but ran light-footed along the balcony, leapt a nine-foot gap to the next, and alighted soundlessly. He threw something up on to the gutter of the neighbouring roof and in six seconds was across the slanted tiles, away . . . For hours we scoured the district, but our quarry had vanished among the chimneys. All I had seen was the glint of a diamond stud in what was obviously a dress-shirt front.

The Inspector was scathing. "You really must forgive me for intruding upon your beautiful part-nership," he said. "But I would like to know about all this before it happened, so we could have one or two more men on the scene – " Upon me he cast a withering glance. "You say you saw him – but you can't describe him – except he climbed like a cat – he didn't have fur by any chance?"

Afterwards I said solemnly: "Tommy, we've got to catch that blighter – that cat-burglar – and rub butter on his paws!" That was not all I said.

We went to the scene of the previous night's burglary. Jewels valued £2,000 were missing, which didn't make us feel better. By daylight that leap from one balcony to its neighbour seemed no less remarkable. We measured it, Tommy throwing the end of a tape-measure across the space to me. And as I leaned to catch it I noticed something . . .

It was a footprint on the balcony ledge – so small and so exquisitely pointed in the toe that it might have been made by a woman's dancing shoe. We got a ladder and in the soft mould of the drainage gutter on the roof found another imprint of the wedge-shaped shoe, the smooth tiles showing clearly the porous tread of crêpe soles. "Rubber-soled evening pumps!" said Tommy. "He'd need to get those made specially!"

I spent the day visiting those exclusive shoe emporiums of Jermyn Street, York Street (as it was then), Dover Street and Shepherd's Market, where craftsmen took pride in hand-made shoes to suit clients' whims. In Albemarle Street I was lucky.

"Most remarkable," said the proprietor earnestly, "that any gentleman should require crêpe rubber soles, however thin, on patent-leather evening shoes. I remember strongly advising the gentleman against it – but he was insistent." The order-book showed name and address as: "R. Radd, 52, Half Moon Street. Five guineas – paid."

A good address. I went to Half Moon Street, but the numbers stopped at 42, and there had never been a 52. A stranger to the district would have been unlikely to know that. It seemed worth investigating the bars and lounges around Half Moon Street. Those were the days of evening clothes for gentlemen in London's West End, so my laundry bill became staggering . . . and the days passed.

More than a week afterwards I walked into the Range Bar. My dress shoes clacked like sabots on the polished parquet corridor. A man passed me. He

wore good evening clothes, a diamond sparkled in
his laundered shirt-bosom, and as he walked it
occurred to me that his feet were making no noise
at all! I glanced quickly – and saw tiny pointed toes . . .
Outside he hesitated at the taxi-rank, then decided to
walk. I jumped into the cab at the tail of the rank.

"I'm a police officer. Follow that man. Don't put
your flag down. I'll lie on the floor."

We rolled after the man with the pointed shoes –
round the corner from Half Moon Street, up another
side street, then: "He's gone into No. 43, Gov'nor,"
said the taxi-driver.

"Right," I said. "Don't stop. Keep going to New
Scotland Yard."

I took the lift to the Criminal Record Office, but
there they knew nothing about the address. I
searched some picked photo files. There was no
record on the man. Still . . . back at Vine Street I
made a report.

For two days we trailed our man without success.
Then he strolled down to Hatton Garden, met a man
in a café, and went with him in a taxi to Southgate,
where they entered a comfortable-looking private
house. After about twenty minutes the man with the
pointed shoes came out alone. I left a colleague to
make inquiries at the house and followed him back
to No. 43.

In a brown van a concealed spark morse receiver
buzzed and stuttered: "Inquiries at house in Southgate – occupier known – admits receiving jewellery –
has just paid £800 – jewellery answers description of
part proceeds from Park Lane thefts."

That did it. We called at No. 43, and a middle-aged
woman answered the polished bell and regarded us
haughtily. She was dressed pompously in rustling
black, and a black taffeta ribbon at her throat held a
cameo brooch.

"Have you a man living here . . .?" I described my
suspect. The woman considered me as though she
suspected some fault with the drains.

"That may well be Mr Delaney, who has the
upstairs flat. Is he expecting you?"

I brushed past her. "We'll just find out!" I called

cheerfully from the stairway.

She gasped, "I think you're very rude!"

So did Mr Augustus Delaney, as his engraved name-plate described him, who looked up coolly as we entered without knocking. "What the blazes do you want?" His accent was slightly Canadian.

"Quite all right," I said, soothingly. "We're just looking for some money and jewellery. You don't mind, do you?" He stood up, suddenly pale, and then his mouth twitched into a wistful smile. "I suppose – it's too much to hope that you gentlemen are burglars?" The £800 was hidden under the mattress. Stolen jewels were concealed in the dressing-table, behind the drawer backs.

On his first conviction he received three years' penal servitude at the Old Bailey for those six Park Lane burglaries. That was in 1924. Would you like to know what this daring, well-educated and quick-witted young man did with the rest of his life and with that superb acrobat's body that fate had given him? By the time he died in Parkhurst Prison on 14 December 1948, he had spent twenty years in various gaols. In his brief intervals of freedom his pointed, immaculate shoes had scarcely time to become worn down at the heels!

The Count of Gramercy Park

Gerald Chapman, the "man prisons couldn't hold", the crook who wore tailor-made suits and spoke with a near-impeccable English accent, was regarded by the American public as a modern Robin Hood, and accordingly lionized. One writer speculates that his parents were comfortably off and that he had a good education. It was all untrue. Chapman was born in Brooklyn in 1890, of Irish parents, and had the usual criminal apprenticeship of petty theft and reformatories. When he was fourteen a judge prophesied he would end in the electric chair. In fact, he was hanged.

It was when he was eighteen, and was transferred from Sing Sing to Auburn, N.Y., that Chapman met a man he came to admire passionately, George "Dutch" Anderson, a graduate of Heidelberg and Uppsala Universities, who spoke several languages. (His real name was Ivan Dahl von Teller, and he was a Dane.) Anderson was a swindler and a "gentleman crook", and he advised Chapman to give up armed robbery and use his brains. Chapman began to educate himself with books and acquired an English accent.

Released from prison, he went back to robbery, and this time was so successful – for a time – that he was able to buy himself expensive clothes, rent a fashionable apartment, and dine in good restaurants. He decided that being a gentleman suited him. But in 1911 he received ten years for armed robbery, and was sent back to Sing Sing. There he became friendly with a man named Charles Loerber, who was in for armed robbery, and who was totally lacking in any kind of finesse.

In 1919, Chapman, Anderson and Loerber were all paroled. Chapman joined Anderson on a tour of the Midwest, and was soon convinced of the soundness of Anderson's methods when they managed to acquire a fortune of $100,000 through confidence trickery. Chapman rented an apartment in New York's exclusive Gramercy Park. Here he called himself G. Vincent Colwell, and acquired a pretty English "wife" called Betty, who was as much a born lady as he was a born gentleman.

It was Charles Loerber who persuaded Chapman to return to armed robbery. He had been observing the mail trucks on Wall Street, and noted that they had minimum security, and that their wire-mesh sides gave a good view of the amount of mail they were carrying.

On the cold, foggy night of 14 October 1921, Chapman, Anderson and Loerber, driving a stolen black touring car, followed one of these post office vans along Wall Street, which becomes deserted after the offices close. Suddenly Loerber accelerated and pulled alongside the mail van as it halted at a red light. Within seconds, Chapman was on the running board, holding a gun to the driver's ribs. This was the dangerous part, when someone might have seen him and given the alarm; fortunately, no one did, and he pulled open the door and sank into the passenger seat. The driver, Frank Havernack, obeyed his instructions to pull over into a quiet side street – Leonard Street. The stolen car pulled up behind them, and Anderson demanded the keys to the van. Then, while Chapman sat with his gun in the driver's ribs, Anderson and Loerber located five sacks of registered mail and tossed it into the car. They drove off leaving Havernack tied up, with a mail bag over his head.

In a hideout across the river – a farm belonging to an uncle of Loerber's – they opened the sacks, and counted out the money and bonds. It amounted to $2,643,720 – the biggest haul so far in American criminal history. More than three hundred thousand of this was in cash, and more than twice that amount in traveller's cheques.

While the police were searching frantically for leads, and Federal agents kept a watch on all the ports, G. Vincent Colwell was back at 12 Gramercy Park, throwing parties to which his wealthy neighbours were invited. He even organized the theft of an expensive pearl necklace from one of his guests. Then the driver identified Chapman and Anderson from "mugshots", and their pictures appeared in "wanted" posters in every post office. But still no one thought of looking in Gramercy Park. Chapman, impeccably dressed, with a neat moustache, often stood in front of the wanted poster, and reflected how little this rough-looking character looked like Vincent Colwell.

Prohibition had arrived. Chapman and Anderson invested some of their money in the bootleg business, and prospered. And in another robbery at an American Express office in Niagara Falls, the gang added a further $70,000 to their capital.

Loerber was their undoing. He was picked up while trying to "fence" some of the securities, and gave away his associates in exchange for a lighter sentence. On 3 July 1922, Chapman and Anderson were arrested. But while Chapman sat alone with a detective in the Federal Building on Broadway, he pretended to have some kind of attack, slumping in his chair and gasping for water. As the detective rushed out of the room, Chapman rushed out of the window, ran along a narrow cornice – his hands shackled – and climbed in at another window. But he was soon located and re-arrested. The escape attempt made the headlines, and Chapman was delighted to see himself described as a modern Robin Hood.

In the Atlanta penitentiary, faced with a twenty-five-year sentence, Chapman swore he would escape. The governor assured him he wouldn't. But with immense patience, Chapman stole small pieces of cord from the workshops and braided them into a rope, which he buried in a flower bed. From stolen cutlery he made a file and a crude hook. Then he began to

complain of stomach pains. After several days he was admitted
to hospital for observation. There he was placed in a room with
a "trusty" named John Grey. He soon persuaded Grey to join
him in an escape attempt. They filed through the bars, severed
an electric cable – plunging the prison into darkness – then used
a rope of bed sheets to get to the ground. Five minutes later,
both men were over the wall.

Two days later, Chapman was tracked by bloodhounds as he
lay in a field; as he tried to run away, he was shot twice, then
handcuffed.

In a civilian hospital in Athens, Betty came to visit him. She
succeeded in smuggling in a gun, and Chapman used it to force
an intern to give him his white coat. Then, after binding and
gagging the intern, he walked out of the hospital and climbed
into the waiting car driven by a fellow-crook, Charlie Wolfe.
Betty joined him a few minutes later and they drove away – and
vanished.

In fact, they made their way to a hideout in Muncie, Indiana,
where Chapman recovered from his wounds in the home of
Dr Harry Spickerman – a man he had met in Atlanta. Then he
persuaded a farmer named Ben Hance to take him in as a
boarder. There, in January 1924, he was joined by Dutch
Anderson, who made an equally remarkable escape from
Atlanta. Anderson had managed to get himself assigned to
the tubercular unit, and was housed in a tent in the prison
grounds – the notion being that plenty of fresh air would cure
tuberculosis. He and a number of other prisoners had tunnelled
their way sixty feet under the prison yard and wall.

Chapman now stole himself an expensive car from a show-
room in Stanton, and changed the numberplates. Then he and
Anderson drove east, committing burglaries and robberies as
they went along. Their aim was to set up in the counterfeiting
business, but in New Britain, Connecticut, they decided that the
department store of Davidson and Leventhal looked as if it
would be easy to burgle, and that early on Sunday morning
would be a good time, when the safe would be full of
Saturday's takings. They were accompanied by a new confederate, Walter Shean, the spoiled son of a businessman in
Springfield, Mass., who enjoyed hanging around with two
famous robbers.

In the early hours of 12 October 1924, Chapman blew one of
the store's safes with nitro-glycerine; to his disgust, it contained
ledgers and an envelope with a few dollars. And while he was

working on the other safes, the police arrived, alerted by a local livery-stableman, who had become suspicious of the well-dressed men entering a large store at dawn on a Sunday. As two armed policemen blocked the doorway of the room in which he was hiding, Chapman fired, then made his escape, followed by flying bullets. The shot policeman, James Skelly, died on the operating table two hours after Chapman and Anderson had escaped.

When the police arrived in force a few minutes after the shooting, they found Walter Shean dozing in the car, and the incriminating envelope containing a few dollars on the back seat. In the warehouse of Shean's advertising agency in Spring-field, police found a large quantity of stolen goods, including fur coats, oriental rugs and jewellery. There were also firearms. It took a large removal van to transfer all the loot to police headquarters.

It was while going through this loot for the hundredth time that Detective Ed Hickey noticed a loose label on a carpet bag, and steamed it off to reveal another underneath; this carried the name of Dr Harry Spickerman of Muncie, Indiana. Spickerman was the doctor who had cured Chapman's bullet wounds. Hickey and his team moved into the Braun Hotel, opposite the surgery of Dr Spickerman, and waited patiently for two months. And in the lobby of the Braun Hotel, on 17 January 1925, one of Hickey's men noticed a well-dressed man with an English accent buying a newspaper. He immediately recog-nized Chapman. The following morning, shortly after leaving Dr Spickerman's house, Chapman was arrested. He put up a fierce struggle and succeeded in firing one shot before he was overpowered.

When the gun was turned over to the forensic lab, it proved to be the same weapon that had killed officer Skelly. Chapman was extradited to Connecticut to stand trial for the murder. His defence was that he was in Holyoke, Mass., at the time of the shooting, but Walter Shean testified against him. So did his former landlord Ben Hance, on whose premises more incrimi-nating evidence was found. On 4 April 1925, Chapman was sentenced to death. In spite of appeals, he was hanged a year later, on 6 April 1926.

By then, Dutch Anderson was already dead. On 15 August 1925, Anderson and a gunman named Charlie Wolfe sought out Ben Hance and his wife Mary, the farmer who had sheltered Chapman and Anderson; they shot them both in their car. Mary died immediately; her husband died later in hospital – but not before he had named his killers. Charlie Wolfe was quickly arrested, and was sentenced to life for the murders. Anderson moved on through northern Michigan, leaving behind a trail of counterfeit bills. On 31 October 1925, he passed a counterfeit twenty-dollar bill in a cafe in Muskegon, Michigan. The manager called a policeman, who caught up with Anderson a few streets away, and Anderson agreed to accompany him for questioning. Suddenly, Anderson darted away into the crowd; the policeman, Charles Hammond, followed him. In a deserted street, Anderson hid under a loading platform behind an empty factory, and as Hammond approached, shot him down. As Anderson ran out from under the platform and took to his heels, Hammond fired after him and brought him down. Both the policeman and the counterfeiter died.

The Inside Job of All Time: The Rondout Heist

Late on the night of 12 June 1924, mail train No. 57 of the Chicago and Pacific Railroad was just passing through the small town of Rondout, Illinois; thirty-two miles northwest of Chicago. The eleven-coach train was ten minutes behind schedule and the driver had pushed the speed up to sixty-five miles-an-hour to try to make up time. So intent were he and the fireman on keeping the boiler at full steam, they completely failed to notice two intruders entering the engine compartment. The fireman looked up from his shovelling to see the muzzle of a rifle levelled at his head and at the same moment the driver felt a pistol in his back.

"Do as I say and you won't get hurt," they were told. "Put on the brakes then flash your headlight three times." As they coasted to a stop the gunman looked back down the train and shouted: "Now back the train three car-lengths." The driver co-operated, positioning the third mail coach over a level-crossing. Four armed men then jumped from two cars parked on the road and ran to the train, firing into the air like archetypal Mexican bandits.

Showing no interest in the other coaches, the robbers made straight for the one straddling the crossing. They dealt with the mail clerks inside by throwing a tear-gas grenade through the upper window. Then, as the agonized clerks stumbled out the door, two robbers in gas masks stepped forward to ransack the coach.

It was at this moment that the men on watch saw a dark figure approaching along the path that skirted the train tracks. "Who the hell is that?" one demanded.

"I don't know," replied another.

Then someone shouted: "Let him have it." The bandits opened fire and the figure staggered and fell to the ground. The robbers ran to the slumped figure and carried it to one of the cars. From their swearing it was evident that they had accidentally shot one of their own people.

Undeterred, the thieves looted the mail coach then sped into the night. They took with them $50,000 in jewellery, $450,000 in newly issued currency and $1,500,000 in readily negotiable bonds; a neat two million dollars in all.

The police started with little to go upon. The train crew were so frightened they reported seeing twenty bandits in all – far too many to fit into the two getaway vehicles. As such their testimony would stand for little at any trial. This, and the lack of any physical evidence, left the police with only two leads.

The first was the wounded man – if he was still alive – he would be difficult to conceal. The police informers were told to keep their eyes open for any underworld medical activity.

The second was the apparent efficiency of the actual robbery. The thieves had known which of the eleven coaches held the richest plunder and in which mail bags to search most thoroughly. This suggested an inside job.

Fortunately, the Chicago police had an expert in such matters on their staff. He was Inspector William Fahy, on secondment from the investigative branch of the US Post Office. He had been sent to put a stop to the growing influence of organized crime in the dealings of the Chicago Post Office – a role similar to the one in which the gangbusting Eliot Ness was to later bring down Al Capone.

At thirty-six, Fahy had an excellent record. Known as the "Lone Wolf" by colleagues for his habit of working alone, he had caught numerous "inside job" robbers, including "Big Tim" Murphy.

Murphy – both a labour racketeer and popular State Senator – had been involved in several major robberies from the Post Office, but had covered his tracks with great care. However, despite much pressure to drop the case, Fahy eventually secured a conviction and lengthy sentence for the mobster. At the time of the Rondout robbery, Fahy was one of the most highly thought of officers in the city. There was no question of anyone else handling the Post Office side of the investigation.

The case soon took a turn for the better. An informant reported that someone who had "soaked up a lot of lead", was secretly being treated at an address in the North Washtenaw sector of the city. The police arrived and found a badly shot up man attended by a friend. In the pocket of the second man they found $1,500 in brand new bills, just like the ones taken at the train heist. A stake-out at the house over the next twenty-four hours netted two more visitors, one being a well-known bootlegger named James Murray.

Inspector Fahy interrogated the suspects personally and it was not long before one broke. Willis Newton identified the wounded man and his nurse as his brothers Willie and Joe. They, Murray and two men called Holliday and Glasscock – from the infamous St Louis gang "Egan's Rats" – had been in on the robbery. Unfortunately, he did not know the identity of the Post Office informer. Only the "Boss", James Murray, had any contact with this person, Newton said.

The engine driver and fireman easily identified Willis and Joe Newton as being two of the robbers. Then, soon afterwards, the police picked up Holliday and Glasscock as well as a fourth Newton brother called Jessie, who Willis had left out of the confession.

Jessie confessed as well and led the police to his stash of the cash. Investigation of the other gang members' haunts also turned up much of the stolen money. However, the investigation into the criminal informant got nowhere. Then the case took a very surprising turn.

One day, a woman calling herself Nan Ryan walked into the office of Police Captain William Schoemaker. She told him that she was the wife of Jerry Ryan, a man William Fahy had recently arrested for robbery. Convinced of her husband's innocence she had set out to find evidence that Fahy was corrupt. Pretending that she had hated her husband she had started to date the officer – he was apparently totally unconcerned that she might be trying to destroy him.

Eventually her self-sacrifice had paid off. Fahy, when drunk, had complained that she always wore the same dress. She replied that she had no money to buy another and Fahy had said; "You just be patient for a couple more days. I'm going to get $14,000 tomorrow."

Incredulous though they were, the Chicago police had to take the accusation seriously. They had Fahy secretly followed and it was soon realized that he was spending far more than he earned. To settle the matter a fake telegram concerning the undercover surveillance of the bailed James Murray was planted on a detective's desk. As soon as he saw it, Fahy sneaked out and rang Murray to warn him. Fahy had not been informed that the bootlegger's telephone was bugged.

The detective was arrested and charged with aiding and abetting the Rondout train robbers. At the subsequent trial, he and Murray – both insisting on their innocence – were sentenced to twenty-five years each. The other robbers were sentenced to between twenty-five years and a year-and-a-day, depending on their co-operation in recovering the stolen loot. Jerry Ryan, husband of the unofficial undercover agent Nan Ryan, was quietly released without trial.

Of the valuables taken from mail train No. 57, all were eventually accounted for but $14,000 – the sum William Fahy had told Nan he was due to receive.

chapter five

THE AGE OF GANGSTERS

Prohibition, which began in 1919, brought the era of gangsterism to the United States. But at least it also brought prosperity to men like Dutch Schultz, Dion O'Banion and Al Capone, and made bank robbery unnecessary. The repeal of Prohibition in 1933 meant that America was full of out-of-work gangsters. Worse still, the great slump of 1929 brought widespread poverty and misery to the wealthiest nation in the world. The inevitable result was a steep increase in crime. And since banks were the places that held the money, bank robbery became the profession of some of the most ruthless of Al Capone's successors – John Dillinger, Pretty Boy Floyd, Clyde Barrow and Bonnie Parker, Alvin "Creepy" Karpis and the Ma Barker gang. Their story belongs in a volume on gangsters rather than robbers, who regard themselves as a specialized fraternity. But it is worth mentioning that much of their success depended on an absurd law that did not permit police officers to pursue bandits over a state line (ie bank robbery was not a "Federal offence".)

The largest bank theft so far was made at the Lincoln National Bank in Lincoln, Nebraska, in September 1930, which broke bank-robbery records with a haul of more than two million dollars in cash and securities – it actually forced the bank to close down. The man who planned this coup was a remarkable character called Harvey Bailey, who had been a respectable farmer until he returned from the First World War, and became a bootlegger. Trouble caught up with him when he lent his car to four bank robbers and they got caught; he was indicted, and skipped his bail. It was this mischance that turned him into a full-time bank robber – although periodically he tried to retire and live quietly with his family. The Lincoln National Bank robbery was the high point of Bailey's career. After that he became – to his regret – involved with the Barker gang and a bumbling gangster called Machine Gun Kelly, whose ambitious wife Kathryn was determined that her husband should be America's foremost law-breaker.

Bailey made two daring prison escapes. But his downfall came when he was on the run with a wounded leg, and took refuge in the Shannon Ranch, in Paradise, Texas, just after Machine Gun Kelly had kidnapped a wealthy oilman, Charles Urschel. Urschel was released on the payment of a ransom of $200,000 – Machine Gun Kelly overruled suggestions that they should kill him anyway. When de-briefed by police, Urschel was able to help them with a series of brilliant deductions and observations he had made while blindfolded in captivity – in particular, the precise time that a commercial plane flew over the ranch every day. This enabled the police to pinpoint Paradise, Texas. Bailey was captured there, with a $500 bill that one of the fleeing gangsters had given him. It proved to be from the ransom money, and Bailey was sentenced to life in Alcatraz for a crime he had no part in.

When Kelly was finally captured in a hideout in Memphis, Tennessee, newspapers reported that he yelled "Don't shoot, G-men", so coining the popular abbreviation for government agents.

The Rubel Ice Company Robbery

One of the boldest robberies of the 1930s took place on the morning of 24 August 1934 in Brooklyn, New York. Just after noon, an armoured car from the United States Trucking Company arrived to collect cash from the Rubel Ice Company on Bay and Nineteenth Street. Before leaving the vehicle the guards scanned the area; everything looked normal, and one guard entered the building while the other waited outside. At this moment, a kerbside pedlar threw a sack off his cart revealing two machine guns. Other men who had looked like innocent loiterers ran up with drawn guns. In a few minutes, bags of money were transferred from the armoured car to two cars belonging to the robbers. By the time the guard emerged from the Ice Company, the cars were speeding away. The New York police were on the scene within minutes, looking for the two cars, but the gang was already unloading the money at a pier less than a mile away into two waiting boats. The gang took their haul to a New Jersey hideout, and found that they had netted just under half a million dollars. The robbers then split up, taking an oath not to speak of their part in the hold-up.

Two years later, the police began to learn the names of men they believed had taken part in the robbery: John Manning, a top criminal, Joseph Kress, who had stolen the cars, two ex-bootleggers called John Hughes and Thomas Quinn, John and Francis Oley, kidnapper Percy Geary and forger Stewart Wallace. Most of these men were later imprisoned for other crimes, but remained loyal to their oath of denying all knowledge of the crime. John Manning, who was almost certainly the planner, was shot and killed in a gang feud on 6 July 1936.

The Invisible Bank Robbers

For sheer skill and planning, the case of the "invisible bank robbers" remains one of the most memorable in America's criminal history.

These thieves were not gangsters, but cracksmen of unusual ability, high-skilled professionals who burned their way into bank safes with an oxy-acetylene torch. But the real mystery was their apparent ability to walk through solid doors. In the majority of cases, the police were unable to discover how the men had broken into the bank. Moreover, the thieves were able to walk the streets with heavy oxygen tanks, apparently without attracting attention. These abilities led one reporter who worked on the case, Edward Radin, to christen the robbers "the phantoms".

Albert Spaggiari had been a hired gun for a right-wing terrorist organisation and had served in the paratroopers in French Indochina. By 1976, however, he was running a photographic supply shop in Nice, ostensibly a settled man. Yet he was planning one of the biggest and most daring bank robberies ever.

The Société Générale Bank in Nice had an ancient vault, built in the 1900s, and Spaggiari knew that this made it a relatively easy target. He surveyed the bank for hours, looking for a way to get to the vault without having to go through the modern building above ground. One day he saw his chance: a team of city cleaners were leaving the sewer from a manhole in a direct line with the vault. If he could tunnel through the underground masonry into the bank while the vault was locked, he could loot the safe deposit boxes and bullion almost at his leisure.

He recruited accomplices of equally dubious backgrounds, including Gaby Anglade, who in 1962 had tried to assassinate Charles De Gaulle, and Jean Kay, a conman who once cheated a rich industrialist out of 8,000,000 francs.

The tunnel was started in an underground parking facility opposite the bank, and took two months to complete. The diggers worked by the light of a fluorescent strip light attached to half a mile of cable, and Spaggiari catered the excavations, regularly bringing large amounts of food and wine down into the tunnel for his partners.

The tunnel complete, the robbery was carried off on 20 July 1976, France's Independence holiday. The gang moved sixty million francs in cash, bonds and jewellery from the vault, leaving the vault's doors welded shut to delay discovery of the crime. Supposedly the gang found some pornographic photographs belonging to a blackmailer in one of the deposit boxes, and pinned them up all around the vault. They also left a message that read: "Without weapons, without hate and without violence."

By October the police had found some of the stolen bonds being sold by a garage owner in Nice. Following this lead, they arrested Spaggiari at Nice Côte d'Azur airport, where he had just returned from a holiday in New York, Hong Kong and Bangkok.

He remained in custody for only four months. Expecting a fifteen to twenty year jail sentence, he broke free of the court security and dived through a loosely secured window onto the street below. As his defence lawyer shouted: "No! not that!" he was picked up by a waiting motorcyclist and driven to freedom.

The first robbery took place on the night of 19 October 1944, at the Long Island City Savings and Loan Association. But the thieves had either been interrupted, or forced to abandon the job because of defects in their equipment. A hole had been burned neatly through the door of the safe, but the contents remained untouched. And the door of the building was locked, exactly as it had been when the manager had left the previous evening. There were no fingerprints – the police did not expect any, since all burglars wore gloves as a matter of course.

In the days of the D'Autremont brothers, safe-breakers had used explosives – usually nitro-glycerine – or "can-openers", huge jemmies that can rip off a safe door. In 1944, oxy-acetylene was the most sophisticated method.

Twelve days later, the "phantoms" broke into a safe in Brooklyn and removed sugar coupons and rationing stamps; again, there was no sign of forced entry. An almost identical robbery took place in Queens thirteen days later. Twelve days after that, the thieves got away with $11,000 in cash and $5,000 in war stamps; this time they had entered by a rear window. A robbery at another Brooklyn Savings and Loan Association in January was less successful – the thieves got away with blank war bonds. But again, the detectives could find no obvious means of entry.

The police interviewed every bank burglar in New York and eliminated most of them from their enquiries; the rest were kept under surveillance. This seemed to deter the "phantoms"; there were no more robberies for two months, and the next one occurred in Newark, New Jersey; the thieves drove off with the safe containing $7,000, and it was found the next day, with the neat burn-hole that had become the trademark of the raiders. But in March 1945, after the retirement of Captain Richard A. Fennelly, the man who headed the "Safe and Loft" Squad – specializing in safe-crackers – the "phantoms" moved back to New York and committed a series of robberies. Fennelly's assistant, Lieutenant Maguire – now promoted to chief of the squad – decided to keep a watch on all savings and loan associations. It required a vast number of officers, but it seemed to be the only way to approach the baffling case.

One day, two policemen sitting in a car in downtown Manhattan noticed two men standing outside a bank. Neither of the men was a known safe-breaker, but the policemen nevertheless felt they looked familiar. Then one of them remembered: they had seen them a week before near a savings and loan association. One was big and muscular, the other small and slim. Now the policemen watched them enter the building, pick up an advertising booklet, then stand by the door, apparently deep in conversation, while they glanced around the room. After this they strolled across to a restaurant opposite. Within a few minutes, two additional police cars had been summoned. When the men emerged from the restaurant and entered a grey Dodge sedan, a plain-clothed detective strolled past and noted its number.

A check with the Bureau of Identification revealed that it was registered in the name of Stanley Patrek, of Clay Street, Brooklyn. A check with the Motor Vehicle Bureau uncovered Patrek's driving licence, complete with a physical description. The Bureau of Criminal Identification was then able to tell Maguire that Patrek, who had been born in 1915, had a record as a hold-up man. He had been paroled in the previous year. His description indicated that he was the shorter of the two men.

Patrek and his companion were shadowed to a garage in Astoria, and later to their separate addresses. The following day, a plain-clothed detective in an unmarked car saw the heavily-built suspect come out of his apartment building, looking as if he was on a shopping errand. The detective slipped into the building and waited on the stairs. When the man returned, he observed which apartment he entered. A name on the door identified him as Joseph Stepka. He, it seemed, had a criminal record as a burglar as well as a stick-up man.

Now the two men were carefully shadowed; it was the constant aim of the police to make sure they had no suspicion they were under surveillance. If they were suspicious, both had sufficient money from robberies to lie low indefinitely. Both men seemed to be happily married, and spent much time at home playing with their children. But they also spent a good part of most days patrolling the streets and surveying loan association offices. One night, the detectives observed them having dinner with two attractive blondes, and deduced that they were deceiving their wives – the women proved to be a dance-hall hostess and a cigarette girl.

On 28 May 1945, a night of torrential downpour, the men left home late at night and returned to their Astoria garage. Three police cars proceeded to trail them as they drove off in the Dodge sedan. But near the Triboro Bridge, the suspects began

Chicago cops with armored car

to weave in and out of side streets, and the police lost them. The following morning, Maguire learned that the "phantoms" had struck again at the Whitestone Savings and Loan Association, and got away with a safe containing $9,000. Again, there was no sign of forced entry, and the door was locked normally when the manager came to open the bank.

The following day, detectives trailed the two men from bank to bank as they made small deposits totalling $9,000. And when Maguire checked with the banks, he discovered that similar deposits had always been made in the past on days following the "phantom" robberies.

On the night of 1 June 1945, Patrek and Stepka again left home late in the evening and drove to the Astoria garage, lifting a bulky suitcase into the trunk. Once again they were shadowed as they followed a circuitous route to their destination, which proved to be Yonkers. The police lost them again, but eventually found the grey sedan parked not far from the Yonkers Savings and Loan Association on Broadway. For the next three hours they waited in darkness. Then the two men returned, both carrying heavy objects. The police ordered them to halt, and both men turned to run. Shots fired in the air made them change their minds. Stepka proved to be carrying the oxy-acetylene equipment, while Patrek held a briefcase containing more than $15,000.

The two men surrendered philosophically, and admitted that they had no idea they had been under surveillance for months. The Astoria garage proved to contain elaborate and expensive safe-breaking equipment – the most elaborate the police had ever seen.

But although they had been caught red-handed, there was no conclusive proof that Patrek and Stepka were the "phantoms" who had committed the previous robberies; understandably, they preferred to leave this problem to the police. The Astoria garage was studied carefully, and the detective in charge noticed some metal filings on the floor. These were turned over to the Technical Research Laboratory. The safe from the Whitestone Savings and Loan Association, which had subsequently been found abandoned, was also handed over. Under the microscope, the floor sweepings were found to consist of asbestos as well as metal filings, a strong indication that they came from a safe – most safes at that time were fire-proofed with asbestos inside the door, and often in the rear wall. Then samples of the filings and asbestos were compared with samples from the safe by means of the spectroscope. In emission spectroscopy, the sample is placed between two carbon electrodes, and a spark struck between them; the light from the burning sample is then split into a spectrum, whose emission lines are as distinctive as a fingerprint. The spectroscope revealed beyond all doubt that the filings and asbestos came from the Whitestone safe.

The chief mystery remained: how had the phantoms succeeded in walking in and out of locked doors? They refused to say; but a small box in their garage workshop finally revealed the secret. The box contained a well-known make of lock, together with an extra cylinder – the part the key slips into – and a tiny screwdriver. If the lock could be approached from the inside – the side that became accessible when the door was open – the screwdriver could be used to loosen a screw in the cylinder. Once this screw had been loosened, the cylinder could be worked out of the lock by pushing in a key, and twisting it back and forth. Eventually, it could be slipped out of the lock, and another cylinder – to which the thieves had the key – substituted. When the robbery was over, the original cylinder was replaced, the screw tightened, and there was no sign of the substitution.

Another lock in the box, partly sawed away, revealed how the thieves had stumbled upon this interesting secret. One of them had obviously made a scientific study of every make of lock until he found one with this flaw. When the watching detectives had observed Patrek and Stepka engaged in earnest conversation as they stood in the doorway of the bank, they had assumed that the men were simply observing the layout of the place; in fact, Patrek was unobtrusively inserting the screwdriver, using the big man's body as cover, and loosening the screw. Here was a case in which the thieves applied to crime the same scientific techniques that forensic experts were applying to their solution. It was a relief for the New York police when both men received long prison sentences for grand larceny.

The Brinks Bank Robbery

Not be be confused with Brinks-Mat, which we shall discuss in a moment, the Brinks bank robbery achieved another record, with a haul of nearly $3 million.

On 17 January, 1950, in the early evening Thomas Lloyd and his fellow employees were checking the day's consignment of cash and cheques. They worked for Brinks Incorporated, the American money-moving firm, in the Boston branch. They worked in the locked wire cage that surrounded the vault, among over three million dollars worth of different forms of money. As they counted and checked, Lloyd was distracted by faint sounds of movement on the other side of the wire. Looking up, he saw seven masked men wearing similar uniforms to his own. Each held a pistol; they were covering all the Brinks staff.

One of the men shouted: "Open up this door. This is a stick-up! Don't give us no trouble."

They had entered the room so quietly that they had given Lloyd and his co-workers no time to reach for the loaded shotguns that rested in a rack by the safe. Thus the Brinks men had no choice but to cooperate.

Lloyd opened the mesh door and, at the gang's command,

lay on the ground with the others. Their hands were bound with cord and their mouths sealed closed with adhesive tape. Over the next twenty minutes the robbers worked hard, stuffing sacks with the money that lay around and also blowing open the vault door with a 20 mm anti-tank weapon. At the end of this time, around seven pm, they left quietly and almost nonchalantly.

It took half an hour for Lloyd to wriggle free of his bonds and activate the alarm. The signal went direct to the police, and they were on the premises by eight. The gang had taken a staggering amount: $1,218,211.29 in cash and $1,557,183.83 in money orders and cheques. Among the haul were bundles of cheques intended for war veterans and half a million belonging to the Federal Bank Reserve. This meant that the robbery was accounted a Federal crime, and soon the bank was filled with FBI agents.

The ease with which the criminals had slipped into the central vault of the holding bank seemed to indicate help from an employee. The locks were intact; somehow the intruders had got hold of duplicate keys for most of the building. Checks on the branches employees revealed nothing, and the police and FBI turned to other methods. They pulled in hundreds of people and questioned them all.

The answer to the puzzling question of how the gang had got in without inside help was actually rather simple. About two years before the robbery, two men, Joseph "Specs" O'Keefe and Stanlet "Gus" Gusciora had been asked by a friend, Anthony Pino, to scout out the Brinks building, with a view to seeing if it was possible to rob it. When O'Keefe and Gusciora checked the bank late one night, they were astounded to find that the outer lock could be turned with only an ice pick, and that the inner doors opened when a strip of celluloid was slid through between the frame and the handle. Using these two simple burglary techniques, the prowlers were able to get right into the vault. There, the alarm was evidently switched on, and the safe door bolted. Hanging on a nail close by was a clipboard with the total amount of money in the vault scribbled on it. The two men let themselves out silently and reported back to Pino.

The main problem, then, was that at the time of day that they could easily use burglary techniques to gain entry, the alarm was always activated. In order to rob the bank, they would have to catch the employees before they left, and this would require a respectable and quiet means of entering the vault. The solution was simple – one night, O'Keefe and Gusciora stole all the locks from the Brinks Incorporated doors and had a fast and discreet locksmith create keys for them. They then sneaked back and replaced the locks well before the morning shift arrived.

Equipped with keys, Pino and associates gathered a group of accomplices and began planning the rest of the crime. They acquired uniforms that resembled the Brinks standard outfit, so that people on the street would not think twice about seeing them loading fat Brinks sacks into their getaway vehicle. Pino ordered that they get some rope, but that it must be stolen so that the police could not trace it. In the event those told to acquire the rope were too lazy to steal it and instead mail ordered it from Sears and Roebuck.

All signs pointed to 17 January being a very busy day for Brinks and consequently a very lucrative day upon which to rob it. Seven men including O'Keefe and Gusciora were detailed to enter the building and commit the robbery while two men, among them Pino, attended the getaway car in the street. One man was to keep watch from a roof top; the final, eleventh man was to dispose of all the evidence that they brought away from the crime, including the truck.

As we have seen, all went very smoothly, and late that evening the gang met to divide up the profits. They gathered at the house of one of the robbers' parents, a couple that spoke no English and were apparently unaware that their son's business activities took place on the wrong side of the law. In a back room the gang divided the usable money from the unusable, which was to be burnt. $98,000 was new, sealed and sequentially numbered, and thus useless without a massive money-laundering operation. Nearly all the cheques and money orders were "trouble money" too, being far too risky to attempt to cash. In all about $1,100,000 was salvageable, making each share worth $100,000. Each of the eleven wandered off into the night rich.

They did not have long to enjoy it however. Within two days all of the eleven had been questioned by the police in their massive sifting operation. Two gang members were given safe-keeping of all the shares, during this difficult time. After they had all been released due to the lack of any evidence against them, $35,000 was found to have disappeared. The keepers maintained that the money had gone while they were being questioned, and thus that they knew nothing about it. Grudgingly the gang accepted this and took back their depleted shares. Soon however the police were back, centring their attention upon O'Keefe. After first removing $5,000 for spending money, O'Keefe handed his money to another gang member, Adolph Maffie, to keep while he and Gusciora temporarily left town.

They set out westward, into Pennsylvania, and it was not long before they began to practise their trade again. They broke into a hardware store and stole five handguns. They then used these to hold up a clothes shop and steal six suits. The fact that there was already FBI and police interest in the pair, coupled with the fact that they were careless, soon led to their apprehension. O'Keefe was given three years, while Gusciora received five to twenty years in prison.

Meanwhile the Boston police had found pieces of the getaway truck in local scrap yards. The gang had intended to bury the sections, but the frozen ground that January had frustrated their efforts. On the strength of evidence gained from examination of the truck parts and also on close observation of some of the gang, the FBI produced a list of eight suspects, including O'Keefe, Gusciora and Pino. As the Statute of Limitations on robbery as a Federal crime means that no criminal can be tried more then three years after the event, the FBI were forced to subpoena the eight men to appear before a Grand Jury in late 1952. They had little chance of success because they lacked solid evidence, and sure enough the prosecution failed early in 1953.

The gang seemed to have escaped punishment; the only chance that the police had was to acquire more evidence and try them under Massachusetts state law. In Massachusetts, the Statute of Limitations occurs only after six years. There seemed little chance however that new evidence would surface after such a long interval, and by the time of O'Keefe's release from jail in 1954, the case was all but closed.

O'Keefe returned expecting to receive his $93,000 dollars from Maffie. Maffie had, unsurprisingly, spent the lot. O'Keefe showed great restraint and did not do anything to Maffie, saying that he could not kill him because he might "get lucky again and pay me back". Instead, O'Keefe tried to extort money from Pino. He kidnapped Pino's brother-in-law and demanded $25,000 from his old boss "for starters". Pino gave him $2,500, and O'Keefe, oddly obliging, gave Pino's brother-in-law back.

His all-but-failed extortion was a mistake in more than one way; soon afterwards his Oldsmobile was sprayed with submachine gun bullets and O'Keefe only escaped injury by flinging himself to the floor. A second attempt on his life left him with gunshot wounds in his chest and wrist. It must have almost been a relief when he was jailed for twenty-seven months on an old offence.

The FBI had heard of O'Keefe's problems, and agents visited him in prison, off-handedly telling stories about the new cars and houses that his old compatriots had been purchasing with their new-found wealth. Within three visits O'Keefe was ready to name his fellow Brinks robbers and testify against them. He was put under twenty-four-hour armed guard, and the remainder of the gang were arrested. O'Keefe's old accomplice Gusciora did not survive to stand trial. While being held in Boston he experienced fits of unconsciousness and vomiting. Within weeks he had died of a brain tumour.

With the testimony of one of the robbers, the rest of the gang were doomed; each received a life sentence. O'Keefe's counsel plead for leniency on the grouds of the help that he had given to the authorities:

"Where would we be – the Commonwealth of Massachusetts or the FBI – if it weren't for Specky?"

O'Keefe was released in 1960. The vast majority of the haul was never recovered.

Hermann Goering, the head of Hitler's Luftwaffe, deserves to be included a book on robbers, since he was one of the most successful art thieves of all time. A member of the German "junker" class and a highly educated man, he was passionately fond of art; so whenever German troops marched into some city with a famous art gallery or museum, Goering had its art treasures sent back to Berlin, many for his own private collection. In late twentieth century currency the value of the plunder would run to billions; even in the 1940s it reached millions.

In 1945 Goering took refuge in Bavaria and tried to take control from Hitler, who denounced him as a traitor. Captured by the allies, Goering was sentenced to death as a war criminal at Nuremberg; he committed suicide by poison before he could be executed.

Emile the Nut

Across the Atlantic, gangsters in Paris and Marseilles were studying the exploits of their American counterparts with admiration. One of these was perhaps France's most notorious and dangerous gangster since the far-off days of the Bonnot gang: Emile Buisson.

Buisson's heredity seems to have been extremely bad. His father was a drunkard, a builder of bakers' ovens, addicted to absinthe. Only four of his nine children survived, and one of them was a weak-minded deaf-mute girl. The two criminals of the family, Jean-Baptiste and Émile, were its only two healthy members; a third brother died of tuberculosis at the age of twenty. The mother, worn out by overwork, starvation, and continual brutal beatings from her husband, was taken to an asylum. The father took to exhibiting his deaf-mute daughter in cafés for money; he was sent to jail for carnal knowledge of minors – including his daughter – and died in an asylum.

Émile was born at Paray-le-Monial, in the Sâone-et-Loire department of southern France, on 19 August 1902. His elder brother fought in the war, deserted, and was sent to a penal battalion in Algeria. Released in 1921, he promptly became a pimp in Paris.

Émile served his first term in jail at the age of sixteen, and then twenty months' imprisonment for theft. He was due for military service, and so sent out to a penal battalion in North Africa. The brutality of these battalions was unspeakable. However, Émile managed to distinguish himself in the fighting, and got the Croix de Guerre. Back in France, he took up a life of petty crime and served many short terms in jail.

In 1932, he helped to rescue his brother from jail. The plan was bold. Jean-Baptiste got himself transferred to Strasbourg model prison at Ensisheim by confessing to a crime in Strasbourg and getting three years added to his eight-year sentence. He there broke his leg by smashing it with a table leg. He was transferred into the hospital, and the same night jumped from a first-floor window, breaking it again. However, with the help of Émile he made a clean getaway.

Émile Buisson committed his first big robbery on 27 December 1937, and got himself the nickname "Mimile le Dingue" – Crazy Mimile. He was driving a "traction avant" Citröen – front-wheel drive (known generally simply as "tractions"), and he and a gangster named Charles Desgrandschamps (known as "Bigfooted Charlie") robbed two bank messengers outside the Banque de France in Troyes. Émile fired at one messenger, wounding him in the thigh, and then, to the surprise of Bigfooted Charlie, began to fire at random down the street and into the bank.

He was arrested a month later. French justice was slow, and in 1940, at the time of the invasion, he was still awaiting trial in Troyes Prison. He escaped. In early 1941, he robbed the Credit Lyonnais bank in Rue Notre Dame des Victoires, Paris, killing two bank messengers in cold blood.

Shortly after this he was caught by the Gestapo carrying arms and sent to a military prison; he was then sentenced for the Troyes hold-up in 1937. He escaped by simulating lunacy until he was transferred to the asylum. In 1947, with four associates, he robbed a café in the Rue Lesueur (site of Petiot's crimes) and later executed one of his associates who kept back a brooch. This gave him such a terrible reputation in the underworld that he was not betrayed by professional informers in the usual way, and stayed at liberty a great deal longer than he might otherwise have done.

Over the next few years he took part in many hold-ups, always using sten-guns and Citröen "tractions". After the war, Paris had become a great deal more dangerous than Chicago in the Prohibition era, and gang killings were commonplace. Finally, the police were armed with sub-machine guns, but after accidentally shooting up an old gentleman who was drunk and a bus full of passengers, they were forced by public opinion to be a little more cautious. Finally, a special bandit squad was formed, adequately financed, and run by Charles Chenevier of the Sûreté, who had arrested Buisson in 1937. There was one unsuccessful attempt to arrest Buisson, when a whole convoy of heavily armed police cars rushed out of Paris towards a hotel at Arpajon; but their spectacular exit from Paris excited attention, and someone phoned Buisson, who escaped. However, he was finally arrested in 1955; and tried for the murder of the gangster whom he had "executed". He was guillotined in 1956.

His brother, Jean-Baptiste, nicknamed "Fatalitas" because of his fatalism, shot a restaurant proprietor, Jean Cardeur, when the latter cast aspersions on his dead brother's memory. Maître Carboni, who defended him, turned to the jury as they filed out and said pathetically: "Do not let me have two heads from the same family on my conscience for the rest of my life." (He had defended Émile.) The appeal was successful; Jean-Baptiste was found guilty with a recommendation to mercy, and sentenced to a life sentence of hard labour in Melun Prison.

Jacques Mesrine: "Public Enemy Number One".

At the time of Buisson's execution, a young Frenchman named Jacques Mesrine was already contemplating a career of crime that was to make him for a while the most famous criminal in Europe. Like so many of his larcenous predecessors, Mesrine liked to think of crime as a way of achieving the fame he deserved, and he revelled in his reputation as a modern Robin Hood.

Mesrine was born in Clichy, Paris, in 1937. In 1940, his mother moved her family to Château-Merle, near Poitiers, where she had been brought up, while her husband was in the army. Mesrine was an attractive child, and his biographer Carey Schofield reports that he was usually able to get what he wanted from adults by smiling at them. But he was also solitary. Once, when asked to go and play with other children, he replied; "No, I always have a nicer time on my own."

After the war, the Mesrines returned to Clichy. Mesrine later claimed that he never had enough affection from his father, who worked hard in a textile designing business. He was a poor student at school, but made a strong impression on his schoolmates with his charm, his prowess at fighting, and his love of argument. His constant absenteeism led to his expulsion from two schools. He began joining other teenagers stealing cars for joyrides. At the age of eighteen, he married a beautiful black girl from Martinique, and they moved into a small flat. But he soon found marriage boring and when his wife had a baby, decided that his mother could bring it up.

At nineteen, Mesrine was conscripted into the army, and asked to be sent to Algeria, where the French were trying to put down a Muslim revolt. There was much brutality on both sides.

Mesrine thoroughly enjoyed being in action, and received the Military Cross for valour. While in the army, he was divorced from his wife.

His return to civilian life was an anticlimax. He soon committed his first burglary. With two other men, he broke into the flat of a wealthy financier. When a drill broke off in the lock of the safe, he went out to a hardware shop, broke in and got more drills. They escaped with twenty-five million francs.

When de Gaulle came to power in 1958, he began seeking a political solution to the Algerian problem. Mesrine, like many Frenchmen, regarded this as a betrayal. The right-wing General Salan set up a secret organization, the Organisation Armée Secrète. Mesrine became involved, and it reinforced Mesrine's attitude to law and order – the typical criminal attitude that it is a question of individual choice and that men who can think for themselves should make up their own minds whether to obey the law.

In the spring of 1962, Mesrine was arrested when on his way to rob a bank, and sentenced to three years in prison. He was released on parole a year later. For a while he decided to "go straight". He married a second time, had a young daughter, and now with his father's help, began to study to become an architect. There is evidence that he was a good architect. But when, in late 1964, he was made redundant, he went back to crime. His cool nerve served him remarkably well. Once, in the course of holding up a jewellery shop, the police arrived. Mesrine ran into the back yard, unlatched the gate to make it look as if he had run through, then hid in a dustbin until the coast was clear. On another occasion, he escaped from a flat he was burgling through a lavatory window, and escaped across the roof-tops, walking out of a building further down the street, and asking the police what all the commotion was about.

In 1967 another attempt to "go straight" as an innkeeper – financed by his father – again proved to be a failure as he found respectability too unexciting. He went off with a woman, Jeanne Schneider, and together they carried out a daring robbery at a hotel in Switzerland. In 1968, as one of the most wanted robbers in France, he decided to move to Canada.

He and Schneider went to work for a Montreal millionaire, Georges Deslauriers, as chauffeur and housekeeper, but the gardener took a dislike to Jeanne, and Deslauriers dismissed them. Mesrine's response was to kidnap Deslauriers, and hold him for a $200,000 ransom. Deslauriers managed to escape before the ransom was paid, and Mesrine and Schneider moved to a small town, Percé, where they made the acquaintance of a wealthy widow called Evelyne le Bouthillier. After an evening spent with the pair, Mme le Bouthillier was found strangled. Mesrine always claimed that he knew nothing about the murder.

They slipped over the border into the United States, but were arrested by a border patrol and taken back to Canada. There they were charged with the murder of Mme le Bouthillier. Mesrine was furious at being accused of the murder of an old woman. He claimed that he *had* committed several murders, and tortured people who had insulted him, but that he would have been incapable of this particular crime. Held in the Percé prison pending trial, Mesrine succeeded in escaping by attacking a guard and stealing his keys. He also released Jeanne. They were recaptured only two miles away. Mesrine was given ten years for the kidnapping of Georges Deslauriers; Schneider was given five. But they were acquitted of the murder of Evelyne le Bouthillier.

A year later, Mesrine led a number of other prisoners in a spectacular escape from the "escape-proof" prison of St Vincent de Paul at Laval. He became a celebrity in Canada and it gave him the idea of a still more daring exploit. After robbing a bank in Montreal, he and another escaped convict drove back to the St Vincent de Paul prison with the intention of freeing the remaining prisoners in the top security wing. But when a police car approached them on the way to the prison, Mesrine opened fire. With bullets whistling past them, they escaped back to Montreal. A week later, Mesrine and two accomplices were in the forests near Montreal where they were stopped by two forest rangers. One of the rangers recognized Mesrine, and made the mistake of showing it. Both were shot down, and their bodies dumped in a nearby ditch and covered with branches.

There were more bank robberies – on one occasion, Mesrine robbed the same bank twice because a cashier had scowled at him as he walked out after the first robbery. Then Mesrine met a beautiful nineteen-year-old, Jocelyne Deraiche, who became his mistress. With two accomplices, they crossed the border again into the United States, continuing south to Venezuela where they were able to live comfortably on the profits of their bank robberies, aided by ex-OAS men living there. When a police official told them that Interpol was on their trail, Mesrine and Deraiche flew to Madrid.

All the publicity he had received in Canada had given

Mesrine a taste for fame. He decided to become the best known criminal in the world. In the remaining seven years of his life, he achieved that ambition.

Back in France, in 1973 Mesrine committed a dozen armed robberies, netting millions of francs. He gathered around him a gang he could trust. As the hunt for him intensified, he made preparations for the future by examining the courthouse at Compiègne. The precaution proved useful. When police finally caught up with him on 8 March, Mesrine staged a spectacular escape from the Palais de Justice in Compiègne, getting hold of a gun that an accomplice had left in a lavatory, then holding up the court, and escaping with the judge as a human shield. He was shot in the arm in the course of his escape, but had the bullet removed when he was safe in a hideout.

Once again at his old occupation of robbing banks and factories, he carefully nurtured the image of the gentleman crook, the modern Robin Hood. When a female bank clerk accidentally pushed the alarm button, Mesrine commented courteously, "Don't worry, I like to work to music", and went on collecting the money. When he heard his father was dying of cancer in hospital, he made a daring visit to see him dressed as a doctor in a white coat with a stethoscope round his neck. Not long after this, a bank robbery went wrong, and the accomplice waiting in the getaway car was arrested. As a result, the police tracked down Mesrine to his flat in the rue Vergniaud and placed him under arrest.

La Santé prison proved to be escape-proof, and Mesrine passed the time by writing a book, *L'Instinct de Mort* (*The Killer Instinct*), which was smuggled out and appeared in February 1977. In it Mesrine admitted that a previous claim to have killed thirty-nine people was a lie, but it contained detailed descriptions of other murders – for none of which a body had been found. After three and a half years, the prosecution finally opened in May 1977. Mesrine astounded the court by telling his audience that it was easy enough to buy the keys that could open any pair of handcuffs, then extracted a matchbox from the knot of his tie and within seconds had removed his handcuffs. The gesture brought him the kind of publicity that he had now come to crave. He was nevertheless sentenced to twenty years.

A year later Mesrine staged another of his spectacular escapes. An accomplice named Francois Besse squirted soapy water into the eyes of a guard, and Mesrine, who was in the interview room with his lawyer, grabbed some guns from a ventilation shaft. Two warders were made to undress, and the convicts dressed in their uniforms. They let another prisoner, Carman Rives, out of his cell, and then all three rushed across the prison yard. Mesrine and Besse escaped over the wall with a ladder, but Rives was shot.

The police commissioner, Serge Devos, was placed in charge of the squad whose business was to recapture Mesrine. Mesrine moved to Deauville, a seaside resort in Normandy. He was unable to resist the temptation of walking into the local police station, announcing that he was a police inspector from the Gaming Squad, and asking to see the duty inspector. They were told he was not there. As they walked out, one of the policemen said, "That's Mesrine", and the other told him that was impossible. Mesrine then robbed a casino in Deauville, and in the desperate chase that followed, was almost caught. After this, he invaded the home of a bank employee who had given evidence against him at his trial, and forced him to go to the bank and hand over nearly half a million francs.

A Paris department store was the scene of another one of Mesrine's typically quixotic gestures in the summer of 1978. He saw the floor-walker seizing a shoplifter – a boy of fifteen. Mesrine announced himself as a police inspector with special responsibility for juvenile affairs, flashing a fake identity card, then grabbed the boy by the scruff of the neck and led him out of the store. There he let him go. In August, he gave an interview to a journalist from *Paris Match*, which caused a sensation. Then Mesrine came to London where he spent several weeks undisturbed by police. There he planned another astonishing crime – to kidnap the judge who had sentenced him to twenty years in prison. On 10 November 1978 Mesrine and an accomplice returned to France, went to the judge's flat and held up his wife, daughter and son-in-law. But the accomplice was inexperienced, and the daughter succeeded in getting word to the judge's son when he came to the door. Mesrine saw the arrival of the police, ran down the stairs, and as he came face to face with several policemen, pointed behind him. "Quick, Mesrine's up there." And they went rushing past. A young policeman who recognized Mesrine outside was handcuffed to a drainpipe.

In hiding, Mesrine wrote an open letter to the French police denouncing conditions in French prisons and claiming that this had "evoked a fanatical passion for human rights". During his last year there was an obvious deterioration in Mesrine's character. "Mesrine believed in his lies more than anyone else did," said his biographer. "Any suggestion, even from his closest friends, that perhaps he was exaggerating a little, could send him into an uncontrollable fury. He had always been subject to fits of rage, and these were becoming more and more frequent . . . He would smash everything that was in his way, and it is extraordinary that he never killed anyone while in a rage." Mesrine explained to journalists – whom he still allowed to interview him – that he now "identified ideologically with the extreme left".

When the police finally located his hideout, in a flat in the rue Belliard, they decided to take no chances. Mesrine had sworn never to be taken alive. On 2 November 1979 Mesrine came out of the building with his girlfriend, Sylvie Jean-Jacquot, and walked towards his BMW, parked nearby. At a road junction, a blue lorry signalled that he wanted to cut across him and turn right. Mesrine waved him on. The lorry stopped in front of the car, and another lorry drew up behind. Four policemen climbed out, and within seconds, twenty-one bullets had shattered the windscreen. Mesrine was killed immediately. Sylvie Jean-Jacquot was shot in the arm, and her dog was also hit. The police flung their arms around one another and danced for joy.

The Great Train Robbery

If Mesrine was the most famous bank robber since World War Two, the most famous single "heist" was undoubtedly the Great Train Robbery. In fact, the *New York Herald Tribune* of 21 January 1964, described it in a headline as "History's Greatest Bank Robbery", followed by the unfathomable comment: "There'll Always Be An England."

On the night of 7–8 August 1963 the mail train travelled southwards as usual, making scheduled stops to load letters and packages into its twelve coaches. Packed into the second coach from the engine on this particular night were 128 large bags filled with paper money, mainly five and one pound notes. The cash had been spent over the August bank holiday that had just passed, and was returning to the head offices of several banks in London. The driver of the train, Jack Mills, and his fireman David Whitby, had taken over the running of the train at Crewe at about midnight. By 2 am they were past Leighton Buzzard in Bedfordshire and were only about half an hour from Euston. Unexpectedly however a signal showed amber rather than green, a sign that the driver should slow down in anticipation of a red signal soon. Sure enough the next signal at Sears Crossing showed red, and Mills brought the train to a halt.

In order to find out what had caused the stoppage, Whitby jumped off the train and made his way to a trackside telephone that was connected to the nearest signal box. The line was dead, the wires having been deliberately severed. Whitby shouted to the driver that the phone had been sabotaged, and ran back towards the engine. As he reached the second coach however a figure stepped from the rear. Thinking that this must be one of the postal workers on the train, Whitby asked, "What's up, mate?" Without replying the figure beckoned him over to the embankment. Suddenly the figure shoved Whitby down the slope where he was overpowered by two waiting accomplices.

"If you shout, I'll kill you," threatened one, holding a cosh

The Great Train Robbery – August 30th 1963 – Mrs Frances Reynolds, Bruce Richard Reynolds, Mrs Barbara Daly and John Thomas Daly are helping with inquiries

over Whitby's head. Panicked, he replied, "All right mate, I'm on your side."

Whitby was taken back to the engine where he found Mills on his knees and bleeding copiously from a head wound. The cab was full of men in boiler suits and balaclavas. The robber who was evidently the train expert was having difficulty operating the engine – it was a new design. Finally Mills, still bleeding, was forced to drive the engine and its first two carriages down the track for about half a mile, to Bridego Bridge where the track goes over a road.

The gang smashed the windows of the second coach with an axe, and overpowered the postal workers inside. All but eight of the bags were unloaded and thrown to a lorry waiting below. Mills and Whitby were handcuffed together and left in the smashed coach; the lorry sped away with over two million pounds.

The police were called from the nearby village of Linslade by two of the postal workers after they judged that the gang were no longer watching the coach. Scotland Yard arrived and began the process of interviewing everyone in the district about new-comers or strange activities.

Within five days, the police had found the gang's abandoned base, Leatherslade Farm, about twenty miles from the robbery location. Neighbours had seen many cars coming and going until up to three days after the crime. They also reported that the windows had been habitually covered while the occupants were at home, and that they had claimed to be decorating the farmhouse. A Mrs Brooke was found, who had actually handed the keys over to the gang so that they could examine it with view to a sale.

The farm was bursting with evidence; almost every surface carried fingerprints. The gang had left a collection of personal objects lying around, including a can of paint, a monopoly set and two Land Rovers with identical number plates.

While the police were cataloguing the bewildering array of clues from the farm, two of the robbers were being captured in Bournemouth. The owner of a lock-up garage on Tweedale Road had become suspicious when the two men had wanted to pay for three months rental in advance with a huge sheaf of notes. While they were moving their van into the garage the owner called the police saying that she thought that she was in the company of two of the Great Train Robbers. Two plain clothes officers arrived and began questioning the owners of the van. Suddenly one of them dashed off down the road.

While the officers were tackling this one, the other also tried to make his escape. Both were recaptured with relative ease and taken into custody. The two men's names were Gerald Boale and Roger Cordrey, and their van proved to be stuffed with money, £141,000 in used notes.

At this point the rest of the gang evidently panicked. Two walkers in Redlands Wood, near Dorking in Surrey, found two holdalls by the side of the path. They were filled with bank notes. Police sniffer dogs also turned up a suitcase around the same location; altogether the bags contained £101,000.

Arrests based upon the evidence from the farm followed quickly, six more men identified by their associates and their carelessly distributed fingerprints. Also the lawyer that organized the sale of the farm to the gang, John Wheater, was charged with conspiracy and the harbouring of Leonard Field, one of the arrested men.

Lastly the police raided the flat of Bruce Reynolds, a man believed to be the organising force behind the crime. The police did not find Reynolds at home, but they did find Roy "The Weasel" James, a man also wanted in connection with the robbery. The police were forced to chase James across the length of St John's Wood before they could capture him. In all, thirteen men had been apprehended.

The trial opened on 20 January 1964, in Aylesbury assize court. The Crown had over two hundred witnesses and a network of circumstantial evidence that seemed incontrovertible. Among the witnesses called to the stand was Jack Mills, the driver of the train. The savage beating that he had received had permanently disabled him; his speech was halting and he had difficulty walking. British Railways had paid him £25 compensation. His evidence was however inconclusive, as he could not identify any of the accused.

Nearly all the defendants had left some fingerprints in Leatherslade Farm and this evidence alone was near damning. Only John Daly successfully overturned the evidence of his prints: his lawyer argued that although they were present on the Monopoly set, the Crown could not prove that they had got there while the set was in the house. He was discharged.

On 26 March 1964, eight of the defendants were found guilty of conspiracy and armed robbery. Three further were found guilty of conspiracy only. The final defendant was Ronald Arthur Biggs, who had succeeded in having his trial held separately from the other men.

The sentencing followed and it was shocking in its severity. Roger Cordrey, who had helped the police extensively, was sentenced to twenty years. All those convicted of armed robbery received thirty years, except Boale, who was given twenty-four years. Brian Field and Leonard Field, convicted only of conspiracy, also received twenty-four years. John Wheater, the gang's lawyer, was treated leniently because of his conduct in the Second World War, and was sentenced to only three years. Appeals were lodged, and in four cases these eventually resulted in reduced sentences.

The press was disgusted with the length of the terms handed down. The *Guardian* described them as "out of all proportion with everything except the value of the property involved". The *Daily Herald* calculated that the prisoners would have been punished less for a combination of manslaughter, blackmail, and breaking a baby's arm.

Three of the gang were wanted at the time of the trial and later tracked down. Bruce Reynolds, James Edward White and Ronald "Buster" Edwards received between fifteen and twenty-five years each upon their eventual capture. Ronald Biggs was sentenced to thirty years in prison, but he succeeded in escaping with Charles Wilson, another of the armed robbers. Wilson was recaptured, but Biggs left the country. He narrowly avoided arrest in Australia, and eventually settled in Rio, where he leads a relatively rich and high-profile life, running his own nightclub and even appearing as himself in Malcolm Maclaren's film *The Great Rock 'n' Roll Swindle*.

The Brinks-Mat Bullion Robbery

In November 1983, robbers in England created another world record.

At 6:40 am on Saturday 26 November 1983, the men of the day security shift had just entered the Brinks-Mat high security warehouse in Houndslow, West London, and were preparing the day's orders. The nondescript factory unit was a stop-off point for valuable shipments travelling to and from nearby

Heathrow airport and contained one of the country's largest vaults. As such, its security systems were state of the art and an undetected entry would have seemed next to impossible.

Nevertheless, as four of the six security guards stood chatting in the locker room a bizarre figure stepped through the entrance. He was wearing a black suit and tie with a trilby on his head. He was also wearing a yellow balaclava and brandishing a 9 mm Browning automatic pistol.

"Get on the floor or you're fucking dead", he roared. Three of the guards complied immediately, but the fourth, Peter Bentley, just stared. The intruder crossed the room and struck him over the head with the weapon, hurling him to the floor with a badly gashed scalp. More armed, balaclavaed men ran into the room and proceeded to bind the guards' arms and legs with tape and to cover their heads with black cloth bags tied at the neck with drawstrings.

The two other guards, Tony Black and Michael Scouse, were in the radio room at the time and were similarly surprised and bound. At this point the man who appeared to be leading the intruders ordered that a radio be tuned to the police waveband to pre-warn them of any alert. The security guards noted that he had a clipped, well-spoken voice with no discernible accent – unlike the others who sounded cockney.

Whoever the raiders were, they knew the Brinks-Mat security systems intimately. The only way to open the vault and safes was with two different keys and two different sets of combinations. These were held by the senior security guards, Robin Riseley and Mick Scouse; the robbers demanded these "keymen" specifically *by name*. Also, on the way to the vault the raiders used *their own key* to open an intervening door.

Outside the vault, Scouse and Riseley were subjected to a fresh incentive to cooperate. Their trousers were cut open and petrol was poured on their bellies and genitals. Scouse was then told: "You better do as I say, or I'll put a match to the petrol and a bullet through your head."

The keymen were given no opportunity to "accidentally" set-off the alarms as they proceeded to access the vault and its safes. The robbers gave specific orders as to which systems had to be deactivated and in what order. This, and other facts, later convinced the police that the criminals had been working with inside information.

Entering the vault they were forced to clamber around a large number of shoebox-sized, grey cardboard boxes to gain access to the three safes. Here the raiders' plan broke down. Riseley had become so frightened he was unable to remember his half of the codes for the safes and no amount of blows or threats could make him remember the numbers.

In frustration the robbers demanded what was in the little boxes. Scouse, realizing that they might kill Riseley if there was nothing to distract them from the safes, replied that the boxes contained gold ingots. Some of the boxes were torn open and the fact was confirmed. In their haste the thieves had almost missed three tonnes of purest gold bullion with an approximate market value of twenty-six million pounds.

Soon afterwards, the other guards – lying in blindfolded darkness – heard the familiar squeak of the loading trolley, the sound of the entry bay doors opening and a vehicle entering. Then they heard one of the robbers shout, "We're going to need another van." Evidently they had come prepared, because another vehicle roared in moments later.

The two keymen were brought back as this went on and one of the robbers sympathetically asked Scouse, "Are you all right, Mick?" Riseley, on the other hand, who the raiders had though was being "a hero", was dismissed with a derisive, "It's a good job it's Christmas."

The vault was emptied and the robbers jumped into the vans. Just as the guards started to relax a little, one of the raiders re-appeared in the doorway. "Merry Christmas!" he shouted, then ran to the departing vehicles.

The six man gang got clean away with £26 million in gold plus £160,000 of platinum, £113,000 worth of rough diamonds and £250,000 in untraceable traveller's cheques. It was the most profitable robbery in British history.

The police had little firm evidence to go upon. The security guards all agreed that the gang was made up of white males between thirty and forty years old, but so were most of the London armed robber fraternity. However, during the hour-long raid some of the thieves had lifted the lower half of their balaclavas to speak more clearly. The guards thought that they might be able to identify the "Bully" and the "Boss", if they saw them again. These were the man who had clubbed Bentley to the ground and the well-spoken leader.

The insurance company that had to shoulder the burden of the robbery issued a £2 million reward for the identities of the thieves, but nobody came forward. The police were left with only one solid line of enquiry, the fact that somebody on the inside of the Brinks-Mat organization seemed to have fed the robbers security secrets.

Although many people had access to this information, there was the fact that the robbers had passed under several security cameras to gain access to the building to consider. This suggested that the two men in the radio room – which also housed the monitors – had not been doing their duty. Interrogation showed that Mick Scouse had been engrossed in organizing the day's shipments, leaving Tony Black to watch the screens alone.

An investigation of Black's background revealed an interesting fact. Although he had a clean criminal record, he was the brother-in-law of Brian Robinson: one of the top ten suspected armed robbers in the country. Robinson's nickname in the criminal underworld was "The Colonel", due to his excellent organizing abilities and military-style, accentless voice.

After intensive interrogation Black broke down and admitted he had been the informant. He had been meeting regularly with his brother-in-law to hand over information, photos of the warehouse security systems and even a copy of the entrance key. Black, thereafter, cooperated fully with the investigation, but in one matter he could not help the police: he had no idea where the bullion was hidden.

The police quickly arrested Robinson and several other suspects. The security guards, at identity parades, singled Robinson out as the "Boss" and a second man, Michael McAvoy, as the "Bully". On 29 October 1984, these two and a third suspect, Tony White, were sent for trial at the Old Bailey under heavy security.

At the trial, Tony Black – who had already been given seven years for his part in the robbery – testified for the prosecution wearing a bullet-proof vest. It was rumoured that the man the press had dubbed "The Gold Mole" had a million pound contract on his head; perhaps the very money he had been promised as his share of the criminal proceeds.

He told the court that neither he or the robbers had any idea that the vault would contain so much loot when they agreed the date of the raid; it had been a matter of pure luck.

Eventually, on 3 December, the trial came to a close. Robinson and McAvoy were both found guilty, but White was acquitted. Outside the court he told reporters: "The evidence against us was the same. We should all have been acquitted." As the judge passed down twenty-five year sentences on

Robinson and McAvoy they both smiled: they had expected life imprisonment.

As the months passed the press interest in what had happened to the king's ransom taken in the raid decreased. It was rumoured that both the gold and the unprosecuted thieves were now safely abroad in countries with no extradition treaty with Britain. The police, of course, continued to investigate with vigour. Such a vast sum of gold was bound to leave some trace of its passing.

Most armed robberies can only hope to net a few thousands of pounds. The safes in the Brinks-Mat vault had held several hundred thousand pounds in used notes on the day of the robbery, and this in itself would have been an excellent haul. Millions of pounds worth of bullion, on the other hand, was quite another matter. The London underworld would not have had the resources to launder such a huge load, so the police began an extensive, national investigation to find those who were handling the gold.

Fourteen months after the robbery, on a freezing evening in January 1985, an incident took place at the Kent country home of wealthy property dealer and businessman Kenneth Noye, which reawakened public interest.

The police had been keeping Noye under surveillance for just over two weeks. They had reason to believe that he was an important link in the Brinks-Mat "gold chain", a group of seemingly legitimate businessmen who were re-casting and selling the gold for the absent robbers. The police team included men from the elite C11 squad – espionage-level experts in covert surveillance – whose job it was to hide as close to Noye's grounds as possible.

On that evening the two C11 officers were Detective Constables John Fordham and Neil Murphy. At 6:15 pm the order was give for them to close in on the house, entering the grounds, to reconnoitre. It has not since been made clear if this was just a standard check of the area or the preliminary to the serving of a search warrant on the Noye property. Either way, the two men were surprised by Noye's young Rottweiler guard dogs and DC Murphy retreated back to the fence. This was standard procedure in such a case and he did not bother to look to see if his partner was following. For some reason though, Fordham continued into the property, despite the barking dogs.

Kenneth Noye heard the dogs and went to investigate. Since darkness had already fallen he first went to his car to get a torch. He also picked-up a kitchen knife, which he later told the police he had been using to scrape clean a battery terminal. He said that as he walked to where his dogs were barking a terrifying figure loomed out of the shadows.

It is true that Fordham would have looked a fearsome sight that evening. He was wearing several thick layers of clothes under a combat style jacket and must have looked huge. He was also wearing a dark coloured balaclava through which only his eyes and mouth could be seen.

Noye stabbed him ten times in the heart region of the chest. He was still conscious when other officers arrived, but was pronounced dead on arrival at Queen Mary's Hospital in Sidcup.

At the subsequent murder trial the prosecution tried to prove that Noye, and another man called Brian Reader, had gone out with the deliberate intention of killing D.C. Fordham. As evidence they produced eleven re-moulded 1 kilo bars of gold found at Noye's house and pointed out to the jury that Reader, who had been visiting the house at the time, was a fugitive from justice – he had been on the run in Spain for some years, trying to avoid a burglary charge at home. To stop Fordham discovering these facts they had, said the Crown, cold blood-edly killed the officer.

Noye replied in the witness stand that he had been unaware of Reader's criminal status. He freely admitted that he was involved in the illegal smuggling of gold bullion, but he was not, he insisted, a murderer. Fordham, he said, had reared up at him in the darkness and struck him across the face. In a panic, and thinking he was about to be killed, he had stabbed wildly at the figure, but it just kept coming towards him. Later he realized that Fordham had been collapsing from the wounds.

Medical evidence showed that Noye had indeed suffered some battering to the face, but could not ascertain if this had happened before or during the knifing. A defence forensics expert also testified that after the killing, Fordham's balaclava had been clumsily tampered with, by persons unknown, to make it look less frightening. This was, presumably, to under-mine Noye's claim to striking out of fear.

In the absence of any immediate witnesses to the killing and the lack of any conclusive physical evidence, the jury found both defendants not guilty. However, Noye had admitted to gold smuggling and thus had little chance of avoiding jail.

He, Reader and a third man, called Garth Chappell, were

later found guilty of conspiracy to handle stolen bullion and evasion of VAT payments. Noye was sentenced to a total of fourteen years imprisonment and was fined £500,000. Reader and Chappell were jailed for nine and ten years respectively.

Since that time the police have failed to retrieve any of the Brinks-Mat bullion or catch any of the other robbers. For a short time a deal was struck with the imprisoned McAvoy and Robinson that if they returned the gold they would greatly increase their chance of early probation; but, in the end, this came to nothing.

The prisoners trusted their associates to keep their shares until they were released, but when they asked for their portions early, they were refused. The authorities offered them a similar deal for the names of the other criminals, but up to now they have maintained the underworld code of loyalty and kept silent.

It is believed that most, if not all the bullion has now been converted into legitimate property and cash and with interest it must now be worth many times the original value of the haul. Much is rumoured to have been invested in London's Dockland refurbishment project.

The identities of the four remaining thieves and many of their associates are now said to be known by the police. They are believed to be living in Spain's Costa del Sol. At the time of writing, August 1993, Britain has no extradition treaty with Spain.

The Knightsbridge Safe Deposit Robbery

Nothing seemed less likely than that someone would break the record established – albeit accidentally – in the Brinks-Mat robbery. But within three years, the gang who robbed the Knightsbridge Safe Deposit had almost doubled it. This may also be regarded as *the* "inside job" of all time, since the man who planned it was the manager and part-owner.

Security Deposits of Brompton Road, Kensington, catered for the kind of customer who found banks a bore. The business provided lockable safe deposit boxes in a secure building and also a discreet lack of curiosity as to their customers' affairs. The owners, Zahid Adamjee and Parvez Latif, had spent £825,000 acquiring the business in 1986, believing that the economic boom of the time would lead to huge demand for high security storage. Things had not gone well however, and in their first year they lost £400,000 and rented out only a quarter of their capacity. Latif stood to lose most, as his background was far less wealthy than that of his partner. He had a £100,000 overdraft, and little prospect of paying it off.

Around this time, Latif became friendly with a client of the firm, a man named Valerio Viccei. Viccei was a conspicuously wealthy young man, with a taste for Ferraris and rich living. He was also wanted in his native Italy, for bank robbery, and was also suspected of involvement with ultra-right wing terrorism. He remained financially afloat in London in much the same way as he had in Italy, robbing banks when he was short of cash. Unsurprisingly, he himself used Latif's business rather than entrust his money to a bank.

The two men socialized, often going to restaurants together. At some stage the fact that Viccei's main skill was the answer to Latif's main problem occurred to them both, and they set about planning the robbery of *Security Deposits*.

Latif increased the value of the business's insurance to £1 million, while Viccei gathered four accomplices and contacted a fence, Israel Pinkas, to help him dispose of any expensive items that the crime might turn up. At around 3 pm, on Sunday 12 July 1987, Viccei rang *Security Deposits* posing as a prospective customer, and asked to be shown around.

That Sunday the business was being run by Latif with only two security guards. One of these took Viccei's call and told his employer that a customer was coming to look at the arrangements. Around 3:15 pm, Viccei arrived with one of his team, and was shown into the secure area by Latif, who all the time was playing the attentive manager eager to acquire a new account. Viccei pulled out a pistol, and in a performance that the police later described as "worthy of an Oscar" Latif "panicked" and allowed the thieves to do what they liked.

Viccei smashed the locks of each box with a sledgehammer, while his accomplice followed with a crowbar and a sack, wrenching open the wrecked doors and grabbing the contents. In the rush, Viccei cut his hand badly, but carried on his work in a very professional manner. At around 5 pm the gang left the building, about £40 million richer.

For the moment however Viccei and the others were not sure of how much they had taken. £2,500 was given out to each of the accomplices as spending money, and the gang split.

It is not known exactly how much was stolen that day. Estimates are low as £20 million and as high as £60 million. Rumours suggested that the gang also got away with some of the laundered money from the Brinks-Mat Bullion robbery two years earlier. The police were, naturally, desperate to apprehend the gang.

The ease with which the crime was achieved seemed to indicate inside help, but for the moment the police did not suspect Latif. He continued his performance, returning to work every morning and trying to deal with the flood of outraged customers.

Some things about the business puzzled the investigating officers. For example there was no video-taped surveillance of the robbery. Latif pointed out, not unreasonably, that many of his customers objected strenuously to being filmed, and that the lack of this security feature was a positive selling point of his service. The absence of any alarm that connected directly to the police was more difficult to explain; Latif's answer to this query was that his staff dialled 999 if there was any problem. For the time being the police were stumped.

Forensic examination of the smashed lockers soon provided a hugely significant clue. There was a fingerprint in blood on one of the doors. The print was so clear and prominent that at first the police imagined that it might be a kind of arrogant challenge from the robbers. Although their attempts to identify the print at first were unsuccessful, searching the records of foreign criminals thought to be in the UK soon produced the name "Valerio Viccei".

Police next set up surveillance on a group of people thought to be Viccei's friends. Among them was Israel Pinkas, who had been very busy since the robbery. Officers observed that some of the group, including Pinkas, frequented White's Hotel on the Bayswater Road. Pinkas seemed often to be looking out for a black Ferrari that regularly parked in the Hotel's drive. The police checked the car's details in their computer, but it showed that the owner was not Viccei.

Observation finally paid off however, and one day the officers recognized Viccei leaving the hotel and climbing into the black Ferrari. Viccei *had* bought the car only a few weeks before, for £87,000 cash. The registration documents had not yet been processed. As the Ferrari pulled into a virtually stationary queue of traffic, an officer tried to reach in through the open window and take the ignition key. Viccei dragged the policeman about twenty yards down the road before another officer succeeded in getting on the car's bonnet and smashing the windscreen with his truncheon. Viccei was under arrest.

Having trapped the man that they believed to be the kingpin of the gang, the police set about following the trails of evidence to his accomplices. While searching Viccei's flat, they came upon an interesting piece of paper: a phone bill from Viccei's room in an Israeli hotel. Among the calls to Pinkas and to other people that the police already suspected was a call logged to Parvez Latif, the owner of the robbed business and supposed victim of the crime. This was damning evidence, and he too was soon arrested, along with Israel Pinkas, Latif's girlfriend and all but two of the rest of the gang.

The trial took place at the Old Bailey, and there was little doubt as to the outcome. Viccei received twenty-two years, Latif eighteen. One of the gang testified against his fellows, and was given only five years. Sixteen months later another gang member, Eric Rubin, was caught and sentenced to twelve years.

The capture of Viccei, and the consequent arrests of the others, could have been avoided entirely were it not for the black Ferrari. Viccei had planned to travel to Colombia and to lie low there. He would not go, however, without his new car. The Colombian embassy were making bureaucratic difficulties, and it seemed that the license to import the car would not be granted for many days. Viccei determined to wait, and in doing so doomed himself and his accomplices to long prison sentences.

The Whitchelo Case

The 1980s witnessed the advent of a new type of crime: consumer terrorism, in which large companies were blackmailed by criminals who threaten to tamper with their products and so cause a slump in their sales. One of the most memorable practitioners of this new dimension in extortion was an ex-police sergeant called Rodney Whitchelo, who was inspired to try consumer terrorism after hearing a lecture about it at the Detective Training School in Ripley, Derbyshire, in the summer of 1986.

Soon after hearing the lecture, Whitchelo – still in the force – opened three building society accounts in the names of John and Sandra Norman. The cash-cards and statements were sent to a mailing address in Hammersmith, so no one ever saw the face of the account holder.

During the course of the next two years Whitchelo was transferred from the Regional Crime Squad to the CID in Hackney; but he took care to keep up with his old mates.

In August 1988, the Managing Director of Pedigree Petfoods in Leicestershire received a tin of his own firm's pet food, together with a letter which demanded £100,000 to prevent its products from being contaminated. The tin of pet food had been injected with poison. If they did not pay, said the letter-writer, dozens of similarly contaminated tins would appear on supermarket shelves. It instructed the company to insert an advertisement in the personal columns of the *Daily Telegraph*.

Pedigree contacted the police, who told them to obey the instructions. So a happy birthday message to "Sandra" was inserted in the *Telegraph*. They added a telephone number suggested by the police.

In a second letter, the blackmailer explained how the "ransom" was to be handed over. It was to be paid into three building society accounts that were in the names of John and Sandra Norman. Here Whitchelo revealed something like criminal genius. Most consumer terrorists, like most kidnappers, were caught during the hand-over of cash. But he could go and draw out money from thousands of cash machines all over the country.

Here the police scored their first minor triumph. Detective Inspector Ian Leacey, who was in charge of the case, authorized some of the money to be paid into only one of the Normans' three accounts – the Halifax. This at least limited the number of machines he could use to nine hundred.

The blackmailer soon began to withdraw cash, at the rate of £300 per day (the maximum). Withdrawals were as far apart as Wales and Scotland. And there was no obvious way to catch the blackmailer except by placing a constant watch on all nine hundred cash machines.

In spite of his success, the blackmailer was furious that the police had restricted him to the Halifax account. He telephoned four supermarkets, warning them that their pet food had been tampered with. Three of the calls turned out to be hoaxes; but the fourth – to a supermarket in Basildon – was not; several tins with minute holes proved to contain injections of salicylic acid. Then he wrote to Pedigree Petfoods again, warning them that in future he would contaminate their tins with razor blades. But Leacey kept his nerve, and declined to authorize payment of ransom money into the other accounts.

In March 1989, Heinz Babyfoods became the target of the blackmailer; they were told that if they failed to pay £100,000 a year for five years, their products would be contaminated with caustic soda.

Now the operation to trap the gang (as the police assumed it to be) was transferred to Scotland Yard, and placed in the hands of Chief Superintendent Pat Fleming. And Fleming decided that he had only one option: to organize a huge operation to watch all nine hundred machines. It would be impossible to mount the watch all the time – the cost would have been prohibitive. But since withdrawals were being made virtually every day, it should be enough to watch all machines on the same day.

The immense operation was a failure. For what Fleming had failed to take into account was that he might be dealing with a blackmailer with "inside" knowledge. Whitchelo had, in fact, resigned from the force in 1988 on health grounds – asthma – but he kept in touch with his old colleagues, who spoke freely in front of him. So whenever detectives – three thousand of them – were engaged in watching cash machines, Whitchelo stayed home. As soon as the operation ceased, he started withdrawals again.

Fleming installed video-cameras at some of the cashpoints. One day, a withdrawal was made at one of these. The tape was rushed to London, and eagerly wound to the right time. The watchers groaned as they saw that the blackmailer was wearing a crash helmet with a tinted visor; he had outsmarted them again.

The blackmailer again tried to force his victims to put money into other accounts. He had so far netted over £14,000, but he wanted bigger sums. Heinz became aware that he was putting on the pressure when a baby in Cowley, Oxford, began to bleed from the mouth as his mother fed him pear yoghurt; the forensic lab found it to be full of tiny fragments of razor blade. A lady in Rayleigh, Essex, was luckier: she had poured

Heinz beef dinner onto a plate for her puppy when she saw a piece of paper that said: "Poisoned with NaOH" in the bottom of the jar. (NaOH is the chemical formula for caustic soda.)

Fleming now tried telling the Halifax to make their machine swallow the card of John and Sandra Norman next time it was presented; they were hoping to get a fingerprint from it. In fact, the card had been handled with gloves; but Whitchelo's response was to threaten to put cyanide in the food. In doing so, he forced Fleming to "go public"; at a press conference on 27 April 1989, he called a press conference and told the reporters about the blackmail. The result, of course, was a slump in the sale of Heinz babyfoods. Oddly enough, it also led to two thousand copycat offences.

Now his account had been closed, Whitchelo's cash supply had been cut off. But when Heinz offered a reward of £100,000 for information about the blackmailer, he saw his chance. He contacted Heinz – using a stencil – and claimed to be someone close to the blackmailers, who would cooperate with the police if the reward money was paid into two building society accounts held in the name of Ian and Nina Fox. Police attempts to trace who opened these accounts were as unsuccessfull as in the case of John and Sandra Norman, which convinced them that this was no informant, but the original blackmailer. Fleming authorised Heinz to pay the reward into the building societies the blackmailer had named.

Fleming was now beginning to suspect that the blackmailer was *too* lucky – that is, that there was some kind of leak. His response was to set up a new and secret operation, code-named Agincourt, and to allow the rest of the force to believe that the cooperation was being run down. Fleming's hunch was confirmed when the blackmailer grew lazy, and began limiting himself to cash machines in and around London. It looked as if he was a Londoner. In which case, he could be caught with a much more limited operation. Fleming's secret group consisted of only enough men to watch fifteen cashpoint machines. The operation was set for 20 and 21 October. Fifteen Woolwich Society cashpoints were staked out, since the blackmailer seemed to favour the Woolwich.

At this point, "Agincourt" was struck by what – at the time – seemed appalling bad luck. A workman with a drill sliced through a cable servicing the Woolwich computer, putting many machines out of action. But since the men were now in position, Fleming decided they might as well press ahead.

Whitchelo had decided on one of his favourite tactics: to go out just before midnight and withdraw £300. Then he could wait until a few minutes after midnight, and withdraw another £300 – the limit being £300 on any specific date.

He chose the machine in Uxbridge, Middlesex. As it happened, this was not covered by a surveillance team. But it was also one of the machines put out of action by the severed cable. Whitchelo drove on to Enfield.

At half past midnight, the surveillance team – of two – at Enfield saw a Peugeot pull up and a man in a crash helmet climb out. They watched him withdraw £300, then stepped up to him as he climbed back into his car. Detective Constable Mark Kiarton asked what the crash helmet was for; the man said that it was raining. Meanwhile, the other constable had found the cashcard in the name of Ian and Nina Fox. "We are placing you under arrest." As he spoke, Rodney Whitchelo slumped in a faint.

Whitchelo pleaded not guilty, but the typewriter on which he had typed the "ransom" demands was found in his bachelor flat in Hornchurch, Essex. So was a tape he had made with a journalist friend with whom he intended to collaborate on a book. Its subject: how to commit the perfect crime.

On 17 December 1990, at the Old Bailey, Whitchelo was found guilty of blackmail and contaminating food products, and sentenced to seventeen years in prison.